Against The Odds

Against The Odds

Major General S. J. Beardsworth

The Pentland Press Limited
Edinburgh • Cambridge • Durham • USA

First published in 1998 by
The Pentland Press Ltd.
1 Hutton Close
South Church
Bishop Auckland
Durham

British Library Cataloguing in Publication Data.
A catalogue record for this book is available
from the British Library.

ISBN 1 85821 560 9

Typeset by CBS, Felixstowe, Suffolk
Printed and bound by Antony Rowe Ltd., Chippenham

For Barbara and the Boys

CONTENTS

ILLUSTRATIONS

FOREWORD BY FIELD MARSHAL THE LORD VINCENT GBE KCB DSO

There are several reasons why I am grateful to Simon Beardsworth for inviting me to write this Foreword. Not least, he worked for me twice in the later stages of his career; and in his typically modest manner he understates the true value and significance of the contribution he made in both appointments, which he held at a time of considerable change and upheaval. Such change was inevitable if we were to move with the times; but its turbulent side effects could have undermined our wider purpose without his steadying hand on the helm. For his understanding always ensured a sensible and practical approach and, above all, it helped maintain the trust and confidence of those involved in these uncomfortable changes.

In a wider context this book also portrays very clearly both the satisfaction of a full and varied career in the Army of his era, and the pressures it put on the families who were constantly being uprooted, or facing long periods of separation. In this regard, Simon and Barbara Beardsworth are a fine example of the commitment and steadfastness shown collectively by so many Service families through the long and demanding period of the Cold War.

Last, but by no means least, this book is also an interesting read because Simon Beardsworth is a man of many parts who, with his family, shares such a wide range of interests. Most of all, he has a very genuine interest in people which is why so many, like me, enjoy reading it.

PREFACE

What follows is an incomplete thing but mine own. It falls woefully short of an autobiography, thank goodness. No one could call it a military memoir in the accepted sense. There is little of the cannon's roar, nor any musings that reflect the experience of high command. I went by another road, and the angle from which I produce my snapshots might be thought to offer a somewhat different slant on service life, both at work and play. This includes my long-suffering family, and other service families will surely read between the lines. That has been part of my aim. If there is entertainment here, I can rest content. I have mentioned many names in passing, and I apologize in advance if I have in any way misrepresented their wholly blameless lives. From those who might be disappointed not to see their names herein, I ask forgiveness for seeming to pass you by. It is why this thing is incomplete.

CHAPTER I

MALTA

There are not many Englishmen, I imagine, who could say that one of their first sentient recollections was of standing by a pillar under the great portico of St Peter's in Rome. I remember it for a very silly reason. Perhaps I should explain how I got there.

My father was a Paymaster Lieutenant Commander in the Royal Navy and had been posted to Malta. The 'pussers', as the Navy call them, do two kinds of jobs. One is to be responsible for all the victuals and stores aboard ship; the other is to fill naval secretarial posts, which in the Army we call staff jobs. My father spent most of his career doing the latter, and in 1934 began a three-year posting on an admiral's staff at Fort St Angelo in Malta.

The plan was for my mother and I to travel by train to Rome where he would meet us. He managed this by travelling from Malta on the admiral's official yacht to Syracuse in Sicily, and then on by ferry and train to Rome. All this was accomplished except that, when we got to Rome, my mother was unwell and had to lie down.

Leaving her in our cabin on the train, my father seized a window in time to visit St Peter's with me, and so I arrived at the pillar. My impression as a five-year-old was of an extremely large church.

This was not a good thing as far as I was concerned. Back home in Petersfield I had disgraced myself regularly at Mass by yelling in protest at 'the ladies singing', whose efforts I judged to be less than perfect. Looking at St Peter's in company with my father, it became clear to my childish brain that the noise inside would be insupportable, and I refused to budge another inch.

My father bade me to remain by my pillar, indeed to put one hand on it, and not move while he went inside to enjoy the marvels within. I can still see him in my mind's eye entering the basilica through those massive doors.

It was thirty-six years before I got back to that pillar, and found my way beyond it into the interior.

The rest of the journey taught me that I was not a good sailor. I took after my mother in this respect. It was no good my father explaining that it was all a matter of getting used to the boat you are in. Oh yeah. In fact, he had to admit it took him a whole day to do that. For example, he said, a destroyer would behave like a bobbing cork, up and over everything. Whereas a battleship would bludgeon through the waves, jerking and juddering with each impact. I found none of this very helpful.

Malta was worth the struggle of getting there. The twin havens of Grand Harbour and Sliema Bay were, and still are, spectacular. The ancient capital of Valetta was carved out of a high rocky promontory dividing the two harbours. There were great caves beneath the town which had provided sanctuary for the population over the centuries, and would do so again during attack from the air in the war to come.

We came to Grand Harbour, the larger of the two havens, through an entrance formed by two long breakwaters, leaving Valetta to starboard, high above us. Across from Valetta, over to port, two big promontories jutted out into the main harbour, providing three more large deep-water moorings. The first, forming an outer harbour, was Bighi Bay. The second was Dockyard Creek, which opened up behind the formidable nose of Fort St Angelo at the point of the first promontory. It was down Dockyard Creek that we were going to live. The third mooring, beyond the second promontory, was called French Creek.

Our home was Number Three Dockyard Terrace, just before one came to the dockyard itself. It might not sound it, but it really was rather grand. We were on the big promontory of Senglea, dividing Dockyard Creek from French Creek. There were six semi-detached houses in the terrace, built into the steep cliff behind. They were three stories high and had large stone balconies on the second and third stories, looking out across Dockyard Creek to the other big promontory of Vittorioso, with Fort St Angelo at its tip. The narrow road leading from the dockyard separated our frontage from the private jetty, where each house owned its own dinghy swinging from davits. At the rear of the second storey there was a large internal kitchen courtyard, giving access to the street behind. The courtyard was overlooked at one point by a balcony in the third storey, which allowed my mother to appear, from time to time, to administer justice if anything untoward was going on among the excitable Maltese staff. Like Lady Macbeth, she used to say.

Our senior member of staff was Tirshie, the cook. He was pretty good. Even I can remember a pièce de résistance for a dinner party given by my parents which involved little white yachts on a green sea with toast for sails. He went regularly to market for the household, and used to display his purchases to my mother in the drawing room. Quite often the final item would be a live cockerel wrestled from the bottom of Tirshie's sack, to be taken away and slaughtered in the kitchen courtyard. I was not supposed to witness this, but of course I did.

One day he very cleverly removed the neck of a large carboy to make an outsize vase for my mother's flower arrangement in the drawing room. I imagine he must have scored the neck with a chisel or something first, but then caused the glass to crack in a neat circle by filling the carboy with water and then inserting a red hot poker into the neck.

The two stewards were Manuel and Lorenzo, or Lorry as we called him. While Manuel was relatively placid, Lorry could overdo things, like the way he leaped to attention whenever addressed by my father. This was often done while disregarding the dangerous angle of the tray that might be in his right hand, filled with teetering cups or glasses. My father could never resist this, and it became a party piece at dinner parties. With guests suitably primed beforehand, my father would wait until Lorry had got outside the dining-room door with the coffee cups. Then he would shout, 'Lorry!'

'SIR!' C-R-A-S-H!! Collapse of guests into uncontrollable giggles, while the mortified Lorry could never decide whether to pick up the pieces or stand to attention again. We loved him dearly, and he was always very kind to me. All three of the male staff appeared to have been locally recruited by the Royal Navy. I think Tirshie was a Leading Seaman, while the others held the rank of Able Seaman.

And then there was Nanny, who was very young. I had never had a nanny before and, frankly, did not want one. My mother soon realised this, and changed her duties to those of a housemaid. She was a nice girl, and I went on calling her Nanny.

We lived in a style never to be repeated, and my mother often used to say that these were the happiest times in her life.

The great delight for a five- or six-year-old was to observe the Mediterranean Fleet in all its glory. In those days it was far, far bigger than the whole of the Royal Navy as we now know it in the nineties. When the buzz went round that the fleet was coming in, we would try to get ourselves to a suitable vantage point. Best of all was to take the picket boat down Dockyard Creek and across the wide expanse of Grand Harbour to the quayside below Barracca Gardens. These were at the top of a high cliff on the immediate outskirts of Valetta. We gained access by means of a large clanking lift rising externally up the vertical face of the cliff. The view from the top was quite impressive.

Perhaps the destroyers would come first, two whole flotillas of them, one for Sliema Bay and one for Grand Harbour. It was important for destroyer captains to enter the harbour with a decent bow wave, and attempt a skid turn when they reached the appropriate mooring, always supposing they were due to anchor in a place where this could be done. Sometimes they had to submit to the ignominy of having a tug push them up the creek somewhere.

While all this was going on, a couple of squadrons of cruisers approached in line ahead and, just breasting the distant horizon, one could see the great foretops of the battleships. Perhaps the cruisers would anchor in line ahead in Grand Harbour, pointing out to sea, leaving room for the majestic leviathans as they began to take up their moorings in a parallel line-ahead formation. And there behind them, destined for Bighi Bay, would be an aircraft carrier and perhaps a battlecruiser. Meanwhile, Sliema Bay would be filling up with a couple of flotillas of submarines and the Royal Fleet Auxiliaries.

But the battleships were for me. These bore many famous names such as *Barham*, *Nelson*, *Ramillies*, *Resolution*, *Revenge*, *Rodney* and *Warspite*. I was small and they were huge and I was in awe of them. Best of all were the children's parties held aboard one or other of the battleships. No one can hold a candle to the Royal Navy when it comes to children's parties. Balloons would be fired out of sixteen-inch guns, there were pirates everywhere, long slides, and voice tubes to blow whistles down before shrilling little messages like 'hello' to the long-suffering yeomen at the other end.

A speciality was a sort of turntable several feet across with a linoleum surface, tapering gently upwards towards a contoured steel plate at the centre, so that the whole thing had a slightly conical shape. A cry would go up for 'all boys aged six and seven', and a disorderly pile of small bodies would form over the central hub. Then a lever would be thrown and the turntable would begin to revolve. As the speed gradually increased, centrifugal force would discharge a steady stream of flailing arms and legs until one small boy was left, clinging like mad to the shiny steel hub. Great fun.

Every dawn and dusk, marine bugles would echo across the water as the white ensigns were raised or taken down. Pipes would wail all day long. Big white awnings appeared over the quarterdecks, and ships began to bring the ladies aboard for parties and dances. It was a glamorous sight to see the admirals' and captains' barges churning about with officers in full rig and their ladies wholly à la mode.

There would be at least one tremendous firework display while the fleet was in harbour, and a searchlight display. I remember a water carnival when every conceivable size and shape of small boat disappeared under a mass of flowers, giving expression to much ingenuity and invention.

Then suddenly, it seemed, all repair work and victualling had been completed, and the whole magnificent vision of the Mediterranean Fleet steamed out to sea again, to the accompaniment of much whooping from the destroyers. With them would go a towed target for gunnery practice, designed like a huge garden trellis. There was also a battered target ship, covered in a dizzy patchwork of heavy armour plate. How it never sank is beyond me.

Return to normality meant a full family life for us, for my father had a job ashore in Malta, diagonally across the creek from us in Fort St Angelo. I learnt to swim in the warm salty waters of Bighi Bay, at Peter's Pool just along the coast, and off the only sandy beaches at Ghain Tuffieha, where one could hire a log cabin for a holiday. I became very confident in a rubber ring, even among quite large breakers at Ghain Tuffieha, a confidence which disappeared rapidly when my parents removed the ring one afternoon in Bighi Bay. I was bidden to swim in convoy with them from the raft to the shore. There was no way one could sneak a toe onto the bottom, which was a good twenty feet beneath me. But what a splendid way in which to learn to swim so young, and the confidence soon came back.

I went to my first school in Senglea on our side of the creek, and promptly fell in love with the senior girl, who must have been about eleven. And I began to learn more about the way of life in Malta. The milkman was in fact a goatherd, and the women would bring their cans to him in the street, where he would milk a goat on the spot. Most of the streets were very narrow, and many of them were just steep flights of steps, usually running in urine from goats and donkeys. So we had to use condensed milk, and a salad or raw vegetables were not allowed.

There was, of course, a 'Malta tummy', and people still seemed to suffer from it in spite of observing the usual precautions with food hygiene. My father cracked it by insisting that we all put on our jerseys as the sun began to go down, even though we might be feeling boiling hot. We never got Malta tummy, and we put it down to this.

We spent a lot of time on the water, sailing to and from Bighi Bay in our little dinghy. And when I graduated to another school in Valetta, I used to go there and back in the dockyard picket boat across the harbour, loving every minute of it. It was a great life for a small boy.

One day the fleet returned, and it happened that the captain of one of the destroyers was due to bring his ship to anchor immediately opposite our house. His name was Donald Bain, and he was a great friend of my parents. He chose that day to ignore the offer of a tug which, quite reasonably, wanted to help him to his mooring in the middle of the creek without touching the sides.

He came in bows first, and began to inch the destroyer round as we watched from our balcony. There were barely feet to spare as the propellers surged, first one way, then the next. So great was the disturbance that quite large boulders were fountained onto our jetty, and our ground-floor basement was completely flooded. Somehow he did it, but he was a worried man, and sent divers down at once to inspect his propellers. There was no damage and he escaped court martial, earning in the process the unswerving devotion of all his crew.

There was a party in our house later, and my father exacted his dues for a flooded basement and a despoiled jetty.

* * *

At the age of six I began to learn about a thing called amateur dramatics. There is a considerable strain of this in our family, and both my parents were excellent actors. The Malta Amateur Dramatic Society was a thriving institution, and its members were privileged to make use of the Opera House in Valetta. I used to watch rehearsals regularly, and in time my mother began to produce plays rather than act in them.

Most communities of any size have a lot of hidden talent, and perhaps service communities more than most. This is not to say that they can act any better, but rather that, through their training, they are generally good communicators and ready to stand up in front and face an audience. They know how to accept direction too, and so some very professional performances become possible.

The key to all this lies in having a good producer, not easy to find in the amateur world. My mother was one such, having plucked up courage in the first instance to have a go. She became rather formidable. Four-stripers quailed under her eye as they turned up late for rehearsal, undoubtedly due to some perfectly reasonable naval exigency which had required their presence.

'And where have *you* been, Captain Blenkinsop, may I ask?'

The hapless lion of empire could only mumble unintelligibly and shuffle onto the stage with his tail between his legs.

My father was always responsible for the programme and poster designs, being a gifted exponent of black and white ink drawings. Naval engineers performed miracles, and one of the best was the famous clock that is central to *Ten Minute Alibi*. The play requires the clock to work in full view of the audience, and at one point the villain steps up to it and adjusts the time by ten minutes. The solution was to make the working parts out of Meccano so that the hands of the clock could be worked manually and patiently from behind by a stage hand. I was sick of some palsy at the time, and the clock was brought to my bedroom for me to play with. It was a great toy, and may have begun the work on my psyche that got me into amateur dramatics myself later in life.

While I escaped Malta tummy, I fell foul of something far worse that made me an asthma victim of sorts for the rest of my life. By that I mean that I grew out of the worst aspects of the affliction after a period of years, but have had to endure a weak 'chest' ever since.

Apparently the villain of the piece was a streptococcus viridens, a name which leaves you and me stone cold, but should be avoided because it is a nasty little bug. The outcome was that my mother and I had to return home to England six months before my father, in the late summer of 1936. We boarded the P&O liner *Rajputana*, and arrived in due course in Plymouth Sound to the accompaniment of mournful hoots from sirens everywhere and a dense, bitterly cold fog.

CHAPTER II

TURBULENT YEARS

Our return to the land of our fathers was masterminded by family, all of whom appeared to be dressed like eskimos. I had absolutely no recollection of how cold it could be in these northern latitudes, and the bug I had collected did nothing to help matters. We spent a short while with my aunt and her distinguished Royal Marine husband in south Devon. Then we migrated even further north to Wrexham. My maternal grandmother was the youngest of a vigorous family of ten, most of whom lived in those parts, so it was decided that we would stay with a great uncle and two great aunts for a few months.

For me this meant a mind-bending two terms at a convent school, where I discovered how much I had yet to learn. The nuns were sweetness itself outside the classroom, and prepared me for my first Holy Communion. But they were tartars in the classroom, and I have never forgotten the anguish of trying to master my multiplication tables in terms of shillings and pence: 'Seven twos are fourteen pence, one and two; seven threes are twenty-one pence, one and nine; etc.' Dreadful.

My father soon returned from Malta amidst much celebration. It transpired that we were to live in Southsea, for he was to join ship aboard HMS *Arethusa*, a cruiser based in Portsmouth. Very soon after this the entire fleet came to fill the Solent as far as the eye could see, and it was like old times, even for an eight-year-old. It was the occasion of the Coronation Review by King George VI and Queen Elizabeth.

On the evening of the great day there came the famous BBC broadcast in which a very tiddly commentator was saying things like 'the fleetsh lit up - all lit up.' It was indeed, for I saw it for myself and gasped at the sheer magnificence of it. Every hull, bridge, mast, funnel and foretop was picked out in electric light bulbs from horizon to horizon. It was a sight the like of which will never be seen again.

We were all gathered on Southsea Common, and a friend of my parents had hoisted me shoulder high. My father, by the way, was aboard ship getting quite tiddly himself. Suddenly the whole fleet went dark as though at the turn of a single switch, and a rather unique and very simple firework display began. The first element of it was a sort of giant golden fountain pouring upwards and outwards from each ship in great globules. And then thousands of rockets were fired in three salvos, simultaneously from every ship - first red, then white, and then blue, lighting up the sky as though it were day.

The other good thing about getting back into naval circles again was the annual children's party at HMS *Vernon*, which was a shore station. Once again we had the turntable and two very big slides and lots of pirates, but there was another miracle of naval engineering to play with. They had a model of a battleship four or five feet long mounted on a table with gun turrets that worked. One could fire real cannon balls across a wooden 'sea' towards the moving target of a little cargo ship about six feet away. If you hit it in the right place, there was a bright flash and it would sink, nose down, very dramatically.

It was about this time that my parents discovered a haven in Cornwall called Lantivet, between Polperro and Fowey, which for many years subsequently became a holiday retreat for the family. It remains unspoilt to this day, for that part of the coast is National Trust. There is just a farmhouse and very few dwellings, and we came to know a marvellous Cornishwoman there called Mrs Leach. Through all the turmoil that was to come, Lantivet was a godsend, and so was Mrs Leach. My mother spent the last years of her life there.

There came a tragedy which concerned my little sister Susan, who was born in 1937 with something seriously wrong in her insides. She had to have an operation, but did not survive it, poor little mite. My mother used to think of her as a cherub in heaven. For my part, I feel quite sure she has been assigned as my guardian angel. No one else could cope.

Meanwhile, I went through two more schools, and then the alarums of war began. More or less coincidentally my father was posted as secretary to the Vice Chief of the Naval Staff (VCNS) on promotion. VCNS was Vice Admiral Sir Tom Phillips who, as a medium-sized officer, was always known as 'Little Tom'. My father had served with him many times before and was quite delighted to be back with him.

In consequence, we moved into a seventh-floor flat in Dolphin Square sometime in the summer of 1939, and my father began work in the Admiralty.

When war broke out, my parents decided that I should be evacuated to Spilsby in Lincolnshire, where I was to remain with my paternal grandmother, a very patient and sweet lady. There was the pressure of yet another school. Only sixpence was needed to go to Saturday matinees at the local fleapit. The sombre voices of Stuart Hibberd and Alvar Liddell emerged every evening from the ancient wireless, as neighbours of my granny came round to share the gloom.

After six months it was decided that, at last, I was to enter a boarding school for the rest of my education. This was to be St Edmund's College, a Roman Catholic school near Puckeridge in Hertfordshire. The preparatory school within the grounds was St Hugh's, and that was where I was due to start. Part of the same establishment was a big seminary for the Westminster diocese called Allen Hall.

I was also to return to London for holidays because, I was told, we were to live in a third-floor flat in Dolphin Square instead of on the seventh floor. It had become a received truth that a third floor flat was the safest place to be if a bomb landed. It would be high enough up to escape shrapnel, and would have the protection of seven very solid floors above. Hence the move, and I could be with my parents again.

The long hard road of boarding school began for me in the summer term of 1940, but unexpected relief came three weeks before term ended. For some happy reason, my mother and I were to join with another woman and her two children for an extended summer holiday of eleven weeks in north Wales. We had known them in Southsea, and now we were to stay in a manor house called Bryn Mally high up in the hills behind Wrexham. It belonged to my great uncle Harry, and stood across the valley from Hope Mountain, above a placed called Ffrith.

Ironically, this was where I heard my first bomb. It was a weekend, and my father was with us. I woke up in the middle of the night to find my parents crouched by my bed making soothing noises. Then I heard the banshee whistles as the bombs descended and the nasty crumps that followed. We soon got used to the fact that the Luftwaffe often missed their way to Liverpool, or perhaps got chased away before they could bomb it. Their solution was to jettison their bombs on the way home. One night, they set nearby Esclusham Mountain on fire and, believing they might have got the Liverpool docks burning, or whatever, they came back to bomb it time and again. The locals never tried to put the fires out. Quite the contrary.

Summer at Bryn Mally was one of those golden times, with many adventurous expeditions to Hope Mountain, carrying our picnic with us. It was still possible to buy bananas, and our favourite treat at the end of a long day was an extraordinary mixture of bananas, golden syrup and currants. On rainy days we romped around the corridors, and on sunny days we enjoyed a place where Pooh, Piglet, Wol and Rabbit might well have been before. Such things always come to an end, and Bryn Mally itself is no more. I have been to look.

Back at St Hugh's for autumn term, we found that all dormitories had been transferred to the ground floor, and the ceilings had been reinforced with the additional support of thick wooden pillars. There was reason in this. A number of serious bangs went off nearby, blowing out some of the windows in the splendid college chapel. We were told they were land mines. So we began a novena to pray for the safety of people and buildings. I suppose we stormed heaven. Anyway, no more bangs occurred until a doodlebug came by a few years later.

When we came out of supper, it was possible to watch a bit of the blitz from the corridor outside the refectory. We could see searchlights waving to and fro, the loom of great fires, and hear the distant boom of guns and bombs. We were never allowed to watch for long, as one or other of the fathers moved us on quickly with a quiet reproof.

After a year in St Hugh's, I was pushed up into the college itself with a number of others, and began my sojourn at St Edmund's in the summer term of 1941.

* * *

I last saw my father as we waved goodbye to each other on Liverpool Street Station at the beginning of the autumn term. Quite soon after, at the behest of Churchill, HMS *Prince of Wales* and HMS *Repulse* were despatched to the Far East. Little Tom flew his flag from the *Prince of Wales*, and my father went with him. They steamed into the South Atlantic and called in at Cape Town. My father sent me a wonderful letter describing his trip with Little Tom to Pretoria to meet General Smuts. I wish I still had that letter.

In due course, as everyone knows, the two great ships set off up the eastern coast of Malaya with neither sea nor air cover. Both sank after an overpowering attack by the Japanese, but many of the crews reached safety on the shore. Of Captain Leach (whose son became an Admiral of the Fleet) there was no news. There was a report of Little Tom sliding down the side of the canting hull, but nothing more. We have seen an airphoto of the bridge of the *Prince of Wales* showing a lone figure in a lifejacket that could have been my father.

He was posted missing first, and then 'missing, presumed killed'. When my much-respected and most excellent housemaster, Father Reggie Butcher, told me the latter, he said, 'Would you like to sit down, boy?'

My reaction was interesting, if not instinctive. 'No, Father. I think I would like to get back amongst the boys.'

I suppose I was groping for some form of normality, and 'the boys' responded magnificently, probably from instinct also.

We were quite close to the end of term, and I believe the school agreed with my mother that I should not go home at once. Just before leaving for the train to Liverpool Street, Reggie Butcher called me in.

'Now, boy. When you meet your mother, tell her how nice she's looking.'

'Yes, Father.'

He was a wise and holy man. When I met my mother, she looked white and drained and exhausted. I did what Reggie Butcher said I should, as best I could. Much, much later my mother told me what a great boost to morale my remark had been for her. But we wept that evening.

In the months and years that followed, normality was a prime requirement, and my mother strove to provide it. There was normality and continuity at school of course, and term-time gave my mother the space in which to earn a living. We were quite poor, and the prospect must have been truly daunting.

I needed licking into shape too, and I cannot have been any help at all as a gloomy teenager mooching about the place. I should have been helping to restore morale, and failed far too often. This must have been frustrating for my beleaguered parent, who will have recognized latent talents in me of leadership, intellect and good humour that really needed to come out.

There was wonderful normality in the love and support which came from family and close friends, one of whom was Donald Bain, the dashing destroyer captain who had flooded our basement in Senglea. And there was normality in the practice of our faith which sustained us through thick and thin.

Normality was difficult to find during holidays, for I had to be left to my own devices most of the time. I find it difficult now to piece together precisely where I was in any given year during the War. Turbulence is a good word to describe what happened to just one deprived family among many tens of thousands.

There was the London scene. Mother worked for a time in a hush-hush part of the Admiralty; then in a factory in Chiswick making parts for ships' engines; and then again at Gabbitas Thring, the schools agency. For my part, I remember becoming demoralized with nothing to do except listen to the radio. There was a wonderful swimming pool, but that only took up an hour or so. The breakthrough was a bicycle. I started cycling all over London, finding my way about. To this day, I have quite a taxi driver's expertise in various parts of the capital.

We would always try to meet for lunch. We regularly cased the menu in a small restaurant in Whitcomb Street, off Trafalgar Square. Best of all was getting involved with the big canteen that somebody got going on the ground floor of the National Gallery. I used to serve coffee at the end of the line, as people came in from all over Whitehall and its environs at lunchtime.

Like most young boys, I found a way of amusing myself at the expense of others. The lifts in Dolphin Square always memorized instructions given to them on the way down, rather than on the way up. I would summon both lifts to the top floor, and then programme each one in turn to stop at every floor on the way down, finishing with the basement. Then I took the stairs down to the ground floor to observe the growing crowd as they expostulated at the behaviour of the lifts. It is difficult to express my joy as, having finally loaded both lifts to capacity, they all went *down* to the basement. It was even better when I joined them in the lift myself. After a while, I sensed a few beetling eyebrows bent in my direction as people began to notice that a young lad with a smirk on his face always seemed to be around on these occasions. So I decided to grow up a little and desist.

There was the Amersham scene. We would often stay with kind friends. Their house was in old Amersham, with ready access into the countryside for me and my bike. Sometimes we would put up in a cheap hotel nearby when their house was full, for we relished more than a spark of civilization in their company. Mrs Langley was a stickler about baths, and there was a line painted in the bath to indicate the maximum depth allowed of five inches. She always thanked 'God and the British Navy' before meals. Robert Skene was a wily spin bowler and a director of Gabbitas Thring, which is how mother got that job. Lally Skene was beautiful and gentle.

There was the Lantivet scene for blissful summer holidays, and one marvellous winter (I think 1944/45) when mother decided to spend six months in Polperro. We rented a delightful cottage called Little Green, behind the renowned and picturesque little hotel called the Noughts and Crosses, whose proprietors were well known to us. This was the 'real' Polperro, inhabited only by fisherfolk and artists, with now and then a visitor or two from theatreland, and one or two lucky people in the know, like us.

There was life under the doodlebugs, or V1 rockets, in 1944. One of the early ones got a bit off line and landed not far from school. A month or two later, at a school harvest camp near Baldock, we watched a doodlebug power-dive into a field not far from us. During the same camp, we watched a disaster that came upon two 'flying fortresses' heading for the Continent in tight formation with many other aircraft. Something went wrong, and one plane side-slipped into another. Both came down, one of them blowing up high above us. Only four parachutes appeared out of a possible twenty-two. A day later, we wandered around the wreckage spread over a wide area. We did all the wrong things, and secreted live cannon shells in our pockets. Eventually I handed mine in to the police in Pimlico, who were rather po-faced about it.

For experience of doodlebugs, my mother would have earned a prize. One day while walking near the Embankment, she looked up to see a 'glider' coming silently towards her over the Thames. With great presence of mind, she ran towards it and flung herself down at the foot of the retaining wall. The thing landed quite close and covered her in dust. On another occasion, one of the beastly things suddenly cut out directly overhead. She looked up, and this one was falling like a stone. She threw herself down, and got up a minute later covered in shards of glass.

There came a Sunday when my mother was attending Mass in Westminster Cathedral. A doodlebug droned over and seemed to cut out immediately overhead. She told me that the silence which followed was absolute, except for the voice of the priest. The explosion came, and then a vast expulsion of breath by the congregation. We found out later that the V1 had landed a short distance away on the Guards Chapel in Birdcage Walk, with much loss of life.

The V2 rockets were easier to live with, in a way. After the bang, one could say that it had landed somewhere else, and there was never any anxious anticipation, as was often the case with doodlebugs. When the very first V2 landed, I think in Chiswick somewhere, my mother and I were in a theatre watching *Arms and the Man*. The cast was sensational, involving Laurence Olivier, Ralph Richardson, Nicholas Hannen and Margaret Leighton. After the bang, we all looked at each other and said it must have been a gasworks. I cannot imagine why.

Back at school, I progressed through the School Certificate examinations (the equivalent of O level or GCSE). I began to blot my copybook by disappearing behind the fives courts for a fag, and at one time narrowly escaped expulsion. It was just as well I became a prefect later, because prefects were allowed to smoke in their own common room. I progressed through the ranks of our Junior Training Corps and became a sergeant.

Then along came VE Day, and we seniors were let out into London for the celebrations. It was truly fantastic to be part of the exuberant London crowd on that occasion. There were about twenty of us and, with great presence of mind, we hung on to each others' hands to be sure no one got separated. Somehow, we made it to the centre of Westminster Bridge for the firework display. The hour that was needed to get off the bridge afterwards was quite alarming. The crowd was dense, and no one had any control of movement. Sometimes there was a terrifying swaying of the crowd, and it became vital to stay on one's feet and not to fall.

In the summer of 1946 I took the Higher Certificate (now A level). I passed Chemistry and Maths, but failed Physics. In those days, it was pass the lot or nothing. One could not put a passed exam in the bag, as it were. So I had to start again. I remained at school as the senior boy, but my mother suddenly decided that I should be removed into a crammer to stand any chance of success. Following an icy interview with the headmaster, my mother marched me away.

As my best man remarked some years later, it was make or break at St Edmund's during those war years. Yes, but I am immensely grateful to St Edmund's for the solid and lasting grounding I was given in my Catholic faith. That was something they got right, by the grace of God.

And so, to end these turbulent years, there came the Chelsea scene, and the Somerset scene. With the help of kind friends, my mother had brought us to the hinterland near Chard where, now in my late teens, I could begin to enter into some of the social life. What fun it was. We lived in a lovely old thatched cottage called Potter's Cottage for much of the time, and as guests in other people's homes on other occasions.

There was an extraordinary function that took place every Christmastide in the Dorothy Cafe, Taunton. The names of no less than eight hostesses appeared at the head of the invitation card, and we lived in eager anticipation of its arrival. The thing was that only squashes and mineral waters were on offer, and so a lot of preliminary planning was necessary. The girls all knew the code - whether the drink was to be gin based or rum based, for example. We young lads secreted the appropriate spirits in our overcoat pockets and, on collecting a tray of drinks, would slink into the cloakroom for the necessary mix. Those parties were highly rated and very noisy. The hostesses must have known, but never let on.

And in Chelsea, for the first six months or so of 1947, we lived in a flat in Britten Street. I went to the crammer every day in Redcliffe Gardens, and my mother went to the Cordon Bleu School of Cookery to take a three-month course, which earned her a certificate. Not only did she bring back her experimental goodies for me to taste, but the cook who came with the flat was a major performer on the list of at least one royal household. I fed well.

The crammer gave me a trial Physics exam on arrival, and I scored 29 per cent. They patted me on the back and told me that my head was crammed with formulae that I did not understand. About five months later, they gave me another trial exam and I scored 29 per cent again. In black despair myself, I found that they were still patting me on the back. No problem, they said, your knowledge of Physics is excellent. We just need to sort out your exam technique. This they did for three more weeks. In the actual exam I scored 69 per cent, and passed Chemistry and Maths as well. I began to appreciate good teaching.

I had been deferred from National Service while I took my exams. Now the time had come. I had no thought of permanent military service. I was beginning to look forward to Cambridge if I could get there, and then maybe go into industry. It seems strange, perhaps, that I should not have leapt at the Royal Navy. I had no intention of doing so, even for National Service, and planned instead to seek the glamour of a short spell with tanks. Perhaps being a bad sailor had something to do with it. Or perhaps there was something psychological about it following the death of my father. God knows.

Many years later, when I was close to the end of my service, an old friend of my father's and his wife were staying with us. He must have been in his eighties and was the last remaining link with my father from Navy days. He was kind enough to congratulate me on my career, and then gazing out of our drawing room window, he added, 'Achieved against the odds'.

I knew exactly what he meant. It was Mum, heroine, who had turned the odds around.

CHAPTER III

ROOKIE

My civilian life came to an end high up between the angel's wings on the Victoria Monument opposite Buckingham Palace. Across the way on the floodlit balcony stood Princess Elizabeth and Lieutenant Philip Mountbatten, acknowledging our plaudits on the eve of their wedding. I, poor wretch, was to begin my National Service the following day while everybody else would be enjoying the party on the streets of London.

In due course I heard a rather gravelly voice, 'Would you mind coming down from there, sir, please?'

The voice belonged to a gentleman in a pointed helmet, so I yielded to authority. The bloke between the angel's wings on the other side remained where he was and, amid many jeers and shouts, a constable climbed the monument to make his wishes quite clear. The other chap descended, with rather more brownie points than me, I think.

So I journeyed to Kingston-upon-Thames on 20 November 1947 and, having had my locks shorn by a brutish barber, went moodily to the NAAFI canteen to listen to the distorted sounds being relayed from the Abbey. It was not a good day for this unwilling recruit.

I expressed my wish to join the Royal Armoured Corps, and after a day or so they gave us an aptitude test. I gazed with horror at the numerous disassembled bits lying on the table before me. I was supposed to put them together to form a carpenter's plane, a bayonet plug for an electric socket, etc. The only thing I could do was a bicycle pump. To my amazement, they ordered me to Barnard Castle where I would join a training regiment run by the 12th Royal Lancers. I often wonder what would have happened had I shown more skill.

Now that I was a Trooper, had begun to learn about armoured cars, and could appraise the colourful accoutrements of the 12th Lancers, things began to look up. Life in our barrack room was a bit basic, and the morning routine somewhat rugged in the cold, cold snow. But we fell into a pattern of cheerful camaraderie and began to look forward with optimism to our new and disciplined life. My own self-sufficiency, acquired the hard way, was a bonus which I probably failed to appreciate at the time.

Four of us in our barrack room became identified as potential officers, or POs. One was a keen rider to hounds from Dorset destined for a regular commission in the 16th/5th Lancers. He was responsible as much as anyone for persuading me to become a regular myself. The other two were both national servicemen. One of them now owns a fine property in the Cotswolds. The other I remember chiefly for his outstanding ability to iron a greatcoat.

He charged me a shilling to iron my coat as I prepared for routine guard parade (our weekly wage, incidentally, was twenty-seven shillings and fourpence). A 'stick man' was always chosen and excused duty from the guard that night. Sure enough, my greatcoat did the trick, and earned me a free ticket to the cinema as well as a peaceful night's sleep. David and I went off happily together for a beer that evening.

Anyone who has been taught to use their initiative will confirm that misplaced enthusiasm lies on the other side of the same coin. For example, there was a time when we went home on a 48-hour pass. On my way back during the Sunday I arrived at Taunton to discover that my train through Birmingham to Darlington had been cancelled due to snow. The image of our Sergeant-Major came readily to mind, so I spent my all on a telegram to say that I would probably miss morning parade.

Then I found out that trains to London were running, and I could probably catch the night train from King's Cross. This was duly accomplished, and I turned up heavy-lidded on parade. It was well towards midday when our Troop Corporal leapt out at me from nowhere and fixed me in an armlock.

'Where've you *been*, mate?' he shouted hoarsely. 'I've been looking for you all over. For Gawd's sake, tell me you was on parade this morning? I'm getting a hard time from the Sarnt-Major, all about some bloody telegram you sent.'

Poor chap. I bought him a beer later. My telegram had failed to arrive until mid-morning, and the wretched Corporal Shuter had been accused of falsifying the roll-call. He had been as heavy-lidded as me, and began to doubt his own senses under a severe grilling from the Sergeant-Major.

The POs were put through a two-week course to prepare us for the War Office Selection Board, or 'Wosbee'. When I confessed to my thoughts about becoming a regular, I was despatched immediately on a weekend pass to consult with my mother.

'Good heavens,' she said, when I arrived unannounced on the doorstep of Potter's Cottage. 'What are you doing here?'

'Well, I was sent to talk to you about whether I should become a regular.'

'Yes, I always thought you would. Come in and have some tea, darling.'

And that was that.

I passed WOSB, and landed up at Mons Officer Cadet School in Aldershot. This was where national service officers earned their commission. While there, I was enlisted as a regular and attended the Regular Commissions Board which was just like another WOSB. I got through that, and so became destined for the Royal Military Academy, Sandhurst.

Mons was inhabited by RSM Britten, who claimed to have the loudest voice in the Army. I can testify to that. I was marching at the far end of the parade ground from the RSM, quite close to the band which was going full blast. Even though a jet aircraft flew overhead at the crucial moment, I still heard the command to 'about turn'.

Sandhurst was inhabited by the senior RSM in the Army, an awe-inspiring man of great moral authority. RSM Lord was waiting for us when we arrived, and we began to mind our Ps and Qs. His reputation included the story of how, after being captured late in the War, he took his POW camp by the scruff of the neck and had them doing innovative drill movements, like folding overcoats by numbers. When relief came, the whole camp was on parade at attention. He was awarded the MBE.

Life as a cadet was pretty rigorous, involving much sport, inter-company competitions, military training, academic work, and the achievement of impossible things on the parade ground. A great deal of pride came into what we did, and we learned quite early on that our Company Sergeant-Major (CSM) was actually on the same side as us.

Each of us had at least one bad day during Academy Parade on Saturday mornings. Names would be taken, and misery would ensue. On the day when I blew it, I escaped my deserts because of my long name, and the loyalty of our CSM.

The dreaded accusation came from the Adjutant, distant on his white horse: 'The third cadet from the right in the front rank of the left half of New College - idle!'

The College RSM burst into the usual response, which was to repeat my name and the offence.

What actually happened was: 'SIR! Officer Cadet Bewa-a, Bah . . . Be-hum . . .'

There came no sound from my CSM, who should have repeated my name yet again, thus driving the final nail into my coffin. I determined that my name had not been taken. When we marched off parade, the order came from the College RSM along the lines of: 'You scallywags who lost your names this morning - FALL OUT OVER HERE!'

I continued marching, while all my chums were saying things like 'Simon, for God's sake!' and 'You lost your name, Simon!'

After we had been dismissed, I marched smartly up to the CSM and stamped to attention.

'Sir?'

'Sir!'

'Er - I didn't hear my name called out on parade, did you, sir?'

'No sir. At no time did I hear your name, sir.'

'That's what I thought, sir. Thank you, sir.'

'Right, sir!'

A smart turn to the right and away. Phew.

It was on another Academy Parade that I found myself with head and eyes turned to the right, looking into the wide open mouth of a drill sergeant who was in the process of giving the command 'eyes front'. It was usual for drill sergeants to take a very long time shouting 'eyes', and while he was doing so, I watched a wasp disappear out of sight and into his mouth - and reappear shortly afterwards in some haste. It took me a long time to convince the incredulous sergeant that this had really happened, but he will have dined out on it ever since.

In due course I became a Junior Under Officer, which meant I could dispense with my rifle in exchange for a cane. I earned two more A levels, in Mathematics. I became one of sixteen due to be commissioned into the Royal Tank Regiment, and managed to pass out third in the order of merit. In December 1949, we finally slow-marched up the steps of the Old Building, closely followed by the Adjutant on his horse (which immediately did its business in the hall). We had a splendid commissioning ball, and much enjoyed the idea of having a pip on our shoulders. I had also enjoyed a moment in company with my mother, after the parade, while waiting for lunch. The omnipotent Academy Adjutant drifted past us in his breeches and boots, and as I stiffened to attention, my mother said, 'Hm, *he* needs a haircut!'

On reflection, apart from my induction into the culture, as it were, the only other thing Sandhurst did for me, in the course of intense physical training, was to teach me how to do a cartwheel.

After a joyful Christmas holiday, one was required to attend the Royal Armoured Corps Centre for a few weeks' training before joining one's regiment. One tried to be languid. This was a mistake. There was a time when the Adjutant at Sandhurst had said, in his idiosyncratic way, that it was the privilege of every British officer, from time to time, to receive an imperial rocket. We were given one at Bovington, or was it at Lulworth? No matter. Noses to the grindstone.

We learnt about Driving and Maintenance (D & M), Signals, Gunnery (the latter at the firing ranges at Lulworth), and a smattering of organization and tactics. I discovered that I liked gunnery best. Not before time, we were despatched to our long-suffering regiments. Yet again, we were to be moulded into a new shape, but this time it was for real. For the first time, we were to face the men under our command.

Four of us joined the 1st Royal Tank Regiment together. We were part of 20th Armoured Brigade stationed at Detmold, a biggish town roughly halfway between Dusseldorf and Hannover. Overlooking the town was a long range of wooded hills that rolled away towards Paderborn further south. It was a good place to be.

At last one began to be part of a family, with all its quirks and traditions. I settled into 1 Troop, A Squadron and began to learn my job. It has been said that a Troop is the finest command for a young officer. There are two aspects to this. First, there is the extraordinary intimacy that has to develop between any tank crew of four, built upon trust and understanding. In barracks, there is the proper sense of formality and discipline. Out in the field, and in one's tank, there is an incomparable solidarity that lifts the spirit. One of the best books about such matters is called *Take These Men* by Cyril Joly. He was Adjutant of the First when we first joined.

The second thing about a troop is the sheer responsibility of looking after three tanks, and all the kit that goes into them. But one is amply rewarded. There is a fantastic glamour about rumbling through town and country in a convoy of tanks, and managing to manoeuvre successfully on an exercise without getting lost. It was a vague perception of this kind that had attracted me to tanks in the first place, and in the event I could not have been happier. Except that I frequently got lost.

Many of us kept dogs. My puppy was a cross between an alsatian, a boxer and a labrador. It looked exactly like a beige-coloured bear, and I called him Brumas after a famous polar bear cub in London Zoo at that time. These dogs came everywhere with us, and were hugely spoilt by the troopers. In the turret of a Centurion tank, there was a large basket under the breech of the main armament which was there to catch the spent brass cartridge cases after the gun had been fired. Most of the time we were not carrying ammunition or intending to fire, so these baskets became dog beds. The unassisted way out for the animal was by way of the driver's seat and out onto the front glacis of the tank, provided the gun had been traversed to the rear. When in convoy, Brumas would sit proudly on the horizontal open hatch cover of my commander's station, high above the many appreciative bystanders. It was amazing how, when the entire regiment might be laid out in a tank park on a training area, a dog out foraging would suddenly prick up its ears as its master's tank started up and began to move towards the fuel point. The dog would go sprinting across the intervening hundred yards or so and leap onto the glacis plate, to disappear down past the ear of a laughing driver.

A major event in any year with British Army of the Rhine (BAOR) was the big autumn exercise, usually involving the whole of 1 Corps. Exercise 'incidents' (by which I mean that somebody somewhere will disgrace themselves) were usually more dramatic during the big exercises. Mine was.

One late afternoon on a fine sunny day, my troop was pursuing a retreating enemy towards a T-junction in a small village on the banks of the River Weser. On the way, I foolishly directed my tank through a narrow defile with steep banks, the effect being that one of my tracks came off. This would mean a lot of work for someone, but I had to continue, so I commandeered my sergeant's tank and left him to get on with it. My sergeant's tank had a gun stabiliser fault, so the gun had to remain traversed to the rear and locked in its cradle. The proper thing would have been for the gun to be pointing forward in a warlike manner.

I took the lead (tactically wrong) and arrived with two tanks at the T-junction. The place was swarming with 'enemy' vehicles of one sort or another that the umpires had failed to extricate realistically. I threw a couple of thunderflashes into the road for good measure, reported my position and settled down to wait.

When things had settled down a bit, I became aware of a very senior posse across the road from me. It included a two-star officer whom I discovered later was Major General 'Windy' Gale. I also learnt later that he had led the airborne assault on D-Day, declaiming to his staff the famous speech from Shakespeare's *Henry V*:

'And men in England now abed will count themselves accursed they were not here to fight with us . . .' etc.

Anyway, an umpire Colonel clambered up to my turret and asked if I could leave my tank while I went across to meet the General. I left my operator in charge and, buttoning my 'jeep coat' (a cut-down greatcoat, creating a sort of bum-freezer that was easy to wear inside a tank), I strode over to the General and saluted smartly. He asked me what I was doing, and I replied as best I could, beginning with the divisional mission and ending with my crucial contribution to that enterprise. I mentioned that I had knocked out lots of enemy.

He dismissed me with a friendly pat on the shoulder, and back I went to discover that a dozer tank had been parked in front of my own tank, blocking the way. (A dozer tank has no turret, and a dozer blade is fitted to the front of the hull.) The umpire Colonel was waiting for me with a glint in his eye.

'What are you going to do about that?' he asked gleefully.

'That's nothing,' I replied. 'If this was war, I'd ram it out of the way.'

He jumped down and went to consult with the General. To my amazement, he returned and shouted up to me, 'Go ahead, then.'

'What, ram it, sir?'

'Yes. Go ahead.'

My driver was incredulous. I persuaded him that all the brass out there had given the order, and we had better do our best. At what followed, my one remaining tank commander, Lance Corporal Davenport, parked just behind me, confessed later that he had put his head in his hands. We began to batter the dozer tank, with very little success. By this time the General and all his party had come across to stand close by, and the watching citizenry were by now ten deep.

Suddenly the General exploded, and his wrath was dreadful to behold. I was bidden by the umpire Colonel to jump down immediately. As I did so, I muttered into the microphone to tell my driver to reverse a bit. Unfortunately, I was standing in front of the General at the moment when I should have been telling my driver to halt. In blissful ignorance he continued, and hit the wall behind, knocking part of it down. Meanwhile, the manifest unfairness of all this had caused me to become very angry myself. I was only doing what I had been told.

'You come here,' the General stormed, 'with your gun facing to the rear, and you have the impertinence to tell me that you have knocked out your enemy. And now look what you've done. You are not fit to be a British officer.'

My eyebrows went up.

'Oh, really?' I said, casting caution to the winds.

The General made a very loud noise, put me out of action for six hours, and stormed off.

The Colonel started to tell me about training gunners properly, with one's gun pointed forwards and so forth. I am afraid I gave him a hard time too. When eventually I simmered down, I became appalled at what had happened, and saw my career lying in tatters about me.

It did not help to discover later that everyone from the Commanding Officer downwards thought the whole thing was the funniest thing they'd heard for ages. It seemed to me that no one understood how awful I had been. I sought an interview with the Adjutant and confessed all.

About a week later, I was summoned to the Colonel's office. This is it, I thought. The Colonel looked me up and down and said, 'Never mind the rights and wrongs of your tactics, what really got the General's goat was that you, Second Lieutenant Beardsworth, stood talking to him with your hands in your jeep-coat pockets! I can live with tactical errors, Simon, but I will not have bad manners from any of my officers. Off you go.'

Mea culpa, mea maxima culpa.

There came a time when the Colonel summoned me on quite a different matter. One of the factors that decided me on becoming a regular was that I would be able to pursue my original plan of taking a degree, once I had got my commission. In principle, this would involve a course at the Royal Military College of Science (RMCS) at Shrivenham, near Swindon, leading to an external London degree. With this in mind, I had rather grandly turned down a place at Gonville and Caius, Cambridge while I was at Sandhurst.

However, all the Sappers seemed to go to Cambridge, and I thought there should be no bar against RTR officers going there too. So when I had the opportunity to speak to our senior Colonel Commandant, I asked him about it. Major General Nigel Duncan heard me out.

'A good idea, Simon. Leave it with me, and we'll see what we can do.'

And so it was that I arrived in the Colonel's office one day to find him with pen poised.

'I have an application form here for you to go to Shrivenham in a year's time, and I have to send it off in a day or two. What do you want to do? Go to Shrivenham, or take a gamble on Cambridge coming up? We haven't heard anything from General Nigel yet.'

I made a snap decision and chose Shrivenham. It is the only example I have of a totally unweighted decision which turned out to be quite fundamental. I could have gone left or right, as it were, and in that moment I had mapped out my future life in so many ways. Nor can it be very common for a person to turn down Cambridge twice! The Cambridge option came up eventually, and a contemporary in the Fourth Tanks went in my stead.

Once again I was summoned to see the CO.

'Simon, the Royal Armoured Corps are forming the 66th Training Regiment in Catterick this coming January. I am ordered to nominate three officers for secondment, and since I'm losing you anyway to Shrivenham, I'm afraid you're one of them.'

I was mightily put out, and protested as much as I dared.

'Get out, Simon, before I change my mind!'

I left the First after a bare eight months or so, and returned only when I came back to take command. Life had been full. There had been lots of tennis, and athletics, and swimming. There had been wonderful comradeship, and I had begun to learn about our traditions.

We were a polyglot bunch in Catterick, from many different RAC regiments, which helped to widen our horizons a bit. It also seemed to encourage a fairly riotous social life. This was just as well, for Waitwith Camp where we were stationed was close to being condemned for human habitation, and was razed to the ground a couple of years later. The sheep from off the moors quite often shared our Mess complex, and kept us awake at nights with their guttural bleats. There was the day when the Brigadier came to do his Administrative Inspection and, typical of such occasions, we found a dead sheep in the emergency water tank close to the Officers' Mess. Somebody got it out just in time.

There was an excellent Amateur Dramatic Club in Catterick Camp with its own theatre. This kept me out of a lot of mischief, and I began to discover a certain talent in this field. It also got me close to the General's daughter, because the GOC would often direct plays, and she liked acting too. All was well until, with the General out front in the stalls, I had to kiss this delightful girl on stage. Remembering my passage of arms with that other general in BAOR, I came all over funny - until the General roared, 'Go *on*, boy! KISS HER!!' Lovely.

For three months in the summer, a number of us were sent off under the Second-in-Command to run a summer camp at Hornsea on the Yorkshire coast for various territorial units. This was an extraordinary interlude, involving a number of mixed units. The clifftop was littered with amorous couples every evening as dusk descended. There were endless welcoming and farewell parties, which were usually reciprocated, and we all drank far too much.

I had to keep our simple Mess Accounts, of which I made a complete hash. When we returned to Catterick, I found that all the right numbers had been put in the wrong places. I stayed up one whole night and had it right by dawn. The auditor handed me a sum close to five pounds for me to keep. I have no idea where it came from.

Time went by, and I could hardly wait to get to Shrivenham.

CHAPTER IV

UNDERGRADUATE

A large slice of my halcyon days came in the next three years. It must have been the same for most of us. We all *knew* they were halcyon days at the time, so it is not just a matter of nostalgia. The Royal Military College of Science, or RMCS, was a very pleasant place to be. For a start, there was a great feeling of space. We were not wrapped up in a city.

The college campus lies outside the villages of Shrivenham and Watchfield in the extreme south-west of Oxfordshire. There are clear views across the Vale of White Horse to the rolling Berkshire downs, while the campus itself is full of woodland and open farmland. The ancient White Horse of Uffington is clearly visible, for all the world like some Picasso from the past.

The land used to belong to Lord and Lady Barrington, who lived in a spacious mansion called Beckett Hall. This was now to be the Officers' Mess for 6th Degree Course, which pleased us greatly. The other two Messes were not nearly so attractive, being located in each of two modern, barrack-like buildings at the other end of the campus. An up-market military barracks was built on the Barrington land in about 1936 in the days of Hore-Belisha. It was the intention to house an anti-aircraft artillery brigade there, but this never happened. The War intervened, and other uses were found for 'Shrivenham', as it has always been known.

The history of the college goes back to 1864 when the so-called Advance Class was formed in Woolwich, for the benefit of artillery officers who sought to learn more about the design and manufacture of ordnance. By the mid-thirties, the Military College of Science occupied Red Barracks in Woolwich and served the needs of all arms of the Service. It was evacuated on the outbreak of war, and finally came to its present permanent location in 1945.

Beckett Hall and its surroundings formed a delightfully civilized oasis for us at the Shrivenham end of the campus, somewhat apart from the starkly functional college buildings. Extensive lawns, graced with a number of fine trees, swept down to Beckett lake close by. There was a 'china house' jutting out over the lake, and a white footbridge that led out towards Shrivenham village. There were pleasant walks through the woods, and lots of high-priced ducks.

Inside the mansion, there was a great central hall that reached up about thirty-five feet, ringed by a wide first-floor balcony that led to upper rooms. The hall served as our main dining room, and other spacious rooms on either side rendered service as billiard room, ante-room, bar, breakfast room and, most important, the popular and well-used Ladies' Room. Only the WRAC were allowed to sleep in Beckett Hall. We men enjoyed a short walk across the lawns to our rooms, located in two wings of the nearest teaching block. There was no hardship in that. We were exceptionally lucky, for the joys and delights of the Beckett Mess vanished some years later when it was converted for use as the College library.

There was a bit of a tussle over which degree I should take. The professors and my military tutor said I should do an engineering degree, by virtue of my having four A levels. I was aghast. However, I was rescued by the Director Royal Armoured Corps, who had been our Brigade Commander in Detmold. This was Major General 'Fairy' Foote VC, who accepted my argument that I should not stay away from regimental duty for more than two years. So I was allowed to read for a General Science degree as I had hoped. Engineering degrees took three years, and were much harder work.

We settled very quickly into a pattern of life. One of the things we had going for us was our common ethos as young army officers. The professors got more fun out of us too, because of our relatively mature average age of twenty-three or twenty-four. Moreover, there were the more senior staff courses sharing our Messes, with a lot more of the military ethos and an average age of about thirty-five. They were mostly majors, and they kept us in order. This was just as well, for we had adopted the collective noun of a 'thrash' of subalterns, and did our best to live up to it. It was significant that, when in later years the College opened up the degree courses for young civil servants, the eighteen-year-olds straight from school found life very difficult indeed. Those who survived went on to render great service in the Royal Ordnance Factories and the Research and Development Establishments.

Extra-mural activity was of a high order, carried on under the twin umbrellas of the Athletic Union and the Arts Council. There was everything from astronomy to weightlifting, and basketball to mountain climbing. For my part, I played rugby and tennis, and threw myself into amateur dramatics. There was a favoured pub in Shrivenham called The Prince of Wales which, at that time, enjoyed a somewhat unusual landlord. He was a retired doctor from a flourishing practice in north London who had decided to give up doctoring when he found that he had a slightly dicky heart. His family were delightful and lively, and we often found ourselves taking a turn to help out behind the bar. In truth, the 'Prince' became an extension of the Mess, and the Commandant would often join us by way of the wicket gate in the wall dividing the pub yard from Shrivenham House, which was where the Commandant lived. It was probably built as a dower house for Beckett Hall.

There was a time when I suffered an infection following a painful session with our military dentist, who was nicknamed 'Lightning Lawton'. My solution was to visit the 'Prince'.

'Good morning, Toby,' I said. 'A pint of special and a penicillin jab please!'

I was taken behind the scenes, and a cure was effected.

Toby's family went on to achieve great things. One son became an Air Vice-Marshal, and the other became a distinguished hotelier. As for Toby himself, rumour has it that he went back to doctoring to escape the pressures of looking after the likes of us.

The amateur dramatic society, the choral society and the orchestral society together lay at the heart of the cultural scene in Shrivenham. Students of all ages provided plenty of talent, but the permanent staff and many local civilians were not only more experienced, but provided the key element of continuity. There was constant activity of high quality that managed to achieve the aim of not embarrassing one's friends.

It was a real workshop, where individuals could begin with walk-on parts and, if things went their way, find themselves a year or so later in a leading role. This was my good fortune, and the fun we all had and the successes we enjoyed were most rewarding. In those days the theatre we used was a cinema, housed in a vast Nissen hut. The stage accoutrements were held together by pink string and sealing wax, and would have given the Health and Safety at Work gang heart attacks if they had been around. The fact that it was normally a cinema meant that we could only afford to hire it for four days from the AKC, whose cinema it was. This was challenging, providing only two days in which to get the set and lighting right, and then rehearse on the proper stage. We would give just two performances, and the following evening the Belfordrome, as it was called, had to be a cinema again.

Every year the dramatic society went in for the nationwide one-act festival, which meant getting an act together in the minute surroundings of the Swindon Arts Centre. There would be three offerings each night during the course of a week, and sometimes we would put in two plays. This was real repertory. The mens' dressing room somehow had to accommodate two male casts at any one time, plus two sets of basic scenery and the accompanying stagehands. The preceding party had a timed five minutes to get their scenery off the tiny stage, and our lot would have the following ten minutes to set everything up. It was controlled pandemonium, and we loved it.

The reckoning came at the end of the evening when the adjudicator, usually a woman, would give the critique. This was an art form in itself, wherein one would hear one's individual performance torn apart in the nicest possible way, and our producers would suffer agonies.

There were more relaxed occasions when we non-singing types would be roped in for, say, a Gilbert and Sullivan performance with all the bells and whistles. We might have to hold onto the proverbial spear without dropping it, but otherwise enjoy the fun backstage. I had my come-uppance on the singing front at an Arts Council party one summer. In spite of my protests I was made to sing three verses to a Gilbert and Sullivan tune. This was part of a comic operetta written for the occasion by the librettists amongst us. A distinguished pianist assured me that she would not let me go out of tune. A distinguished bass singer serving as conductor assured me that he would keep me in time with his baton, which was a lavatory brush. In the event I got an encore, to my great dismay, not because I was any good, but because I had achieved the apparently impossible feat of singing a complete verse precisely one semitone out of tune.

I found myself organizing an enterprise called the Gallery Club which, for an astonishingly small sum, took a party of thirty or so by bus to the New Theatre in Oxford for various entertainments. These were often just before or just after a West End production, and ranged from ballet through drama to one wonderful evening with Ruth Draper. After a while, we paid a bit more and took our seats in the dress circle, as well as having bacon and eggs in the Elizabeth Restaurant. These trips were always well attended, sometimes once a month and sometimes three times a month, depending on the programme.

This was just one example of the social culture of the time, which was to make our own life around Shrivenham, rather than to go rushing off to London all the time. We came to mingle our lives quite closely with the teaching staff and civilian friends nearby, accepting invitations into their homes and making real friends in the neighbourhood. Undergraduate life is rather different in RMCS today.

Of course, we did go to London, for there was an immensely cheap place to stay in South Kensington called the Bernhard Baron Club, run by the YMCA. It cost us nine shillings a night for a bed and, in exchange for a further five shillings, one got given a key to the front door. This ensured that one had five shillings in one's pocket at the end of the weekend, which was an important consideration. The whole approach in that club was excellent. One night I arrived without having booked, and while the long-suffering lady behind the desk examined her books, I said, 'I really don't mind going in the cellar, if that will help.'

'My dear man,' she said, looking up. 'You *are* in the cellar.'

One officer on our course had a splendid S100 coupé and, in exchange for the cost of petrol, we would sometimes thunder up to London with him. Many of us took out membership of a small club close to the Bernhard Baron which sported a restaurant, a bar and a dance floor. In this way we could take our ladies out quite cheaply. The routine on Sundays was always the same, though. Without exception, we would arrive at a pub called the Antelope in Eaton Square promptly at noon. This was where we sampled the hair of the dog in amiable surroundings, to round off our infrequent forays into the capital city.

* * *

The entertainments which based themselves in and around Beckett Hall were invariably excellent, simply because of the ambience, and the close-knit mixed community which I have tried to describe and which we enjoyed so much. The wooden surrounds of one of the great doors of the Ladies' Room were adorned with a collection of snipped-off ties that went some way towards rivalling the collection at The Bear Inn in Oxford, giving evidence of many hilarious evenings spent in the Mess.

The Summer Ball at Beckett was a marvellous event, with lots of coloured lights spangled around the trees and lawns, with an illuminated fountain in the middle of the lake, and a large marquee to add to the spacious rooms of Beckett itself. On these occasions we would tend, men and women, to finish up on the high slopes of White Horse Hill five miles away, just to let go our remaining reserves of steam as the sun rose. Then the girls would be delivered back to their weekend hosts, while the men woke up a few hours later in deck chairs out on the lawns, still in dinner jackets, and looking at their watches. The subsequent rendezvous was invariably The Prince of Wales.

These were romantic occasions which, I venture to suggest, were not quite equalled in universities elsewhere, because of our relative seniority and our common ethos. We all thought about things in the same way, I suppose.

There was the business of 'rags', of course. We reckoned we were quite good at this, with a set of rules that said: first, there should be no damage; and secondly, it should still be funny the following morning. The routine way in which we went about this was to build pyramids of furniture after a big dinner in the Mess. By this I mean a thirty-foot-high pyramid in the great hall of Beckett, designed by the sappers among us, and built by idiots like myself. Such a pyramid would start with two big refectory tables laid across two others to form a base. Next came two layers of sofas, followed by two layers of armchairs. It began to be dodgy after this, using ordinary dining-room chairs but, once erected, the edifice was amazingly stable. We were greatly pleased to discover that our batmen regarded these pyramids as a wonderful challenge, and looked forward to dismantling them in fifteen minutes flat the following morning. But, in our own tiddly state, immense trouble would be taken to ensure that not a scratch appeared on any table top, and no sofa torn. Most of the time, we got that right, and so did the sober batmen.

Bigger enterprises were planned as the time came for us to take our finals. On the night of our last celebratory dinner, 6th Degree Course split into two parties. I was personally concerned with the party which planted a 35-foot silver birch neatly in the centre of the Senior Common Room lawn, with a properly etched plaque to say who had done it. The other party went up to White Horse Hill with lots of distemper and turned the white horse itself into a pink and white zebra.

We learnt later that a party from 5th Degree Course had decided to uproot our tree and erect it in the great hall of Beckett. This was an excellent plan, but when they came to our tree the following night, they found that some silly vandals had chopped it down four feet from its base and left it lying there. While deploring this (as we did when we heard about it) they took the shortened tree and erected it as planned. Once again, with sapper advice, the thing was well done. And the batmen took it down with great elan, once everyone who wanted to had taken a good look at the sight of a tree standing free in Beckett Hall.

To my great surprise, I found myself under pressure from my professors to stay a further year to do a Special Physics degree, on the grounds that I was probably going to get a second-class degree in that summer of 1953. This was no big deal really, but I found the temptation considerable, in spite of my pompous assertion two years previously that I should not spend more than two years away from regimental duty. Once again, I had the opportunity to put the problem before the new DRAC, who came to visit the College. He was quite clear with his advice: 'Stay on, my boy,' he said. 'Very good for the Corps.'

So I stayed.

The wastage rate in subaltern WRAC officers at the College was considerable. Not many lasted as much as a year. One by one, they succumbed to the blandishments of some young officer, and were rapidly replaced. The WRAC ran a company at Shrivenham to provide drivers and waitresses mainly, and they were commanded by a captain. Elizabeth Young was in command at the time, and she kept me in the picture over the latest replacement as her second-in-command. This was to be Barbara Bingham Turner, and I met her on 4 August 1953. My life was changed for ever. Mark you, my friends spotted this a fair time before I did, and will have laughed about my condition.

We soon discovered we were both Roman Catholic, and both liked acting a lot. It went on from there, as one might imagine. On 30 November I decided to propose, and on 4 December did so at her parents' home near Beaminster in Dorset. The fact that I can remember these dates is proof enough that I had found the love of my life. My future father-in-law, a retired brigadier from the Gunners, registered his approval unconventionally. 'Well,' he said, 'I'd as soon Barbara married you as anybody.'

Meanwhile, my professors were getting seriously worried. He'll never make it, they said, he'll never pass. My mind was not on the important business of atomic physics and the quantum theory. But they did their best, and by some fluke I got through, although not very creditably, I have to admit. But then, I said to myself, it's all a matter of priority. And we got wed.

I contacted my old squadron leader from my days in the First, who was doing a job in the postings department. The First were due for a spell in Korea as part of the Commonwealth Brigade. Naturally, it would be unaccompanied. I said that if I had to go, of course I would, but it would be nice not to start married life unaccompanied if it could be helped. My point was taken and, rather to my surprise, I was posted to 6 RTR in Munster, Nord Rhein-Westfalen, West Germany.

CHAPTER V

'A MARRIED ADJUTANT'

I was made up to Captain on arrival with the Sixth, which was a lovely surprise. It was only an 'acting' rank, but the increase in salary was real enough and rather timely, I thought. After all, I had a wife to support. In fact, Barbara was still in Beaminster with her parents and would follow me out in about two months' time. So I was able to concentrate on settling in to regimental life again before she arrived. It had been nearly four years since I left the First, and I would have to start all over again with the Sixth.

To my delight and relief, this was not true at all. There were eight 'Royal Tanks' at that time, each with their particular traditions and trademarks, but the ethos was always the same. The same black beret, the same cap badge, the same black denims (unique in the British Army), the same regimental march and the same red, brown and green flag conspired to make one feel at home within minutes of arrival. Even the Regimental Standards (our equivalent to the cavalry Guidons and infantry Colours) were the same, except for the number in the corner indicating which regiment it was. Because of these things one could slide effortlessly back into regimental life as though one had never been away, even though one might be changing one's base, as I was.

Things have not been quite the same for the distinguished regiments of cavalry, particularly in the face of repeated amalgamations over the years. While there exists a long and glorious tradition which all cavalry regiments share, their long histories have moulded them into quite unique, relatively small regiments, each with their own particular ethos. For example, any two regiments of heavy dragoons were quite distinct from each other, and the same went for light dragoons, and for hussars, and for lancers.

In the half-century since I first joined the Army, the story has been one of constant cutbacks and amalgamations between famous regiments. In that time the Royal Armoured Corps has been reduced to some 40 per cent of its post-war strength. We came to learn that it was generally a bit easier for two RTR regiments to amalgamate than, say, two regiments of hussars - or, for that matter, two infantry regiments of the line. This was due in part to the fortunate similarities between RTR regiments, and also because our history is quite short. Our tradition derives from being first into battle with tanks, and became established with the Battle of Cambrai on 20 November 1917, a mere eighty years ago.

This is very different from the cavalry, or the great county regiments of infantry, or the regiments of the Royal Horse Artillery. Most of them have been around for the best part of 300 years or more, and have become deeply embedded in the history of the nation. Of course, the Gunners will remind us that they go back to the invention of gunpowder, and that their traditions are bound up with the battery rather than the regiment. The Royal Engineers, bless them, like to imagine a tradition that takes them back at least to the days of Julius Caesar. But the Sappers have more of a corps tradition than a regimental one. Indeed, the Royal Tank Regiment, as a 'big regiment', used to think of themselves as a corps in the early days, but there is a particularly powerful imperative which comes from having to work within the close-knit harmony of a tank crew.

In fostering our own tradition, we simply have not had the time to develop any significant differences in the way RTR regiments do things. We have found this to be a great help during the painful process of amalgamation and disbandment that has had to be endured. In the course of the last few decades, the Royal Tank Regiment has been reduced to a quarter of its strength, from eight regiments to two. I myself have been amalgamated once and disbanded once, which is pretty well par for the course.

I took up the duties of motor transport officer, or MTO, in Headquarter Squadron. In barracks, this meant looking after all the soft-skinned vehicles which make up what is known as 'first-line' support. This function is a regimental responsibility and, when in the field, Headquarter Squadron organizes three levels of supply behind the so-called 'sabre' or tank squadrons. These are known as A1 Echelon, A2 Echelon and B

Echelon. The MTO usually commands A1, which keeps close up behind regimental headquarters with an immediate supply of fuel, ammunition and water carried in perhaps six trucks. A2 lies much further back and carries the main supplies needed for replenishment each night, including rations and mail. B Echelon carries the regimental baggage left out of battle, and is commanded by the Quartermaster. During most peacetime manoeuvres, B Echelon stays behind in barracks to look after the shop and the needs of all the families housed in the home garrison.

The field exercises with A1 were great fun, with plenty of opportunities for initiative and even panache. The idea was to try and discern the moment when regimental headquarters (RHQ) would suddenly up-sticks and clatter forward to some new location. This had to be done without asking silly questions on the radio in the heat of battle, even supposing one could get a word in edgeways. But one of the best ways for A1 to operate was to scuttle forward and occupy the old RHQ leaguer before somebody else dived in and pinched it. Unfortunately, a 4-ton truck tends to lumber rather than scuttle at the best of times, and the roads are always policed by fierce-looking staff officers and military police trying to keep the route clear for someone or something far more important than you.

After three years of untrammelled university life at Shrivenham, I had no inhibitions about using initiative, and at least one exploit caught the attention of the Colonel (I stole somebody else's bulldozer believing it was ours). Either because of this (which caused him much amusement) or, more likely, to keep me out of harm's way and under his eagle eye, he appointed me as his Adjutant before the end of the year.

Barbara joined me in September, and I carried her across the threshold of 57 Wieganweg in a southern suburb of Munster called Gremmendorf. We were lucky to get a quarter. The Army took the same view as my mother's generation and expected nobody to get married before their twenty-fifth birthday. In those days, one could not qualify for a marriage allowance until the age of twenty-five, and until then had to rely on a bachelor's wage. By chance I had got this right, and we had a Local Overseas Allowance as well to help fill the coffers. Money was fine, and our drink cupboard filled up with all manner of exotica.

But we were still very lucky to get a quarter. Our position on the waiting list depended upon a points system. The longer your service, the higher your rank, the more children in the family, and the length of separation endured in the previous three years all contributed to your score. We were close to zero, but somehow the ebb and flow of families within the garrison went in our favour, and we moved in.

This was when we discovered that the honeymoon was over. It was worse for Barbara. Our barracks was at the opposite end of the city on the northern outskirts, and on the first morning I disappeared in a cloud of dust to leave Barbara staring at four walls and nothing to do and no transport. For a very active girl who had been used to riding vigorously to hounds and the busy life of an officer in the WRAC, this was bewildering. She had a German lady to clean the house for her, which was fine for the company but left her nothing with which to occupy her own time. Besides, the initial language barrier made communication very limited.

Most fortunately, our next-door-neighbours were also from the Sixth, and one of the liveliest couples in the garrison, which was saying something. Jill Barry bounced Barbara out of any undue melancholia, and together they explored the city and the expatriate oasis of the NAAFI. For my part, it was a significant jolt to realize that, at the lunch hour, I was *not* about to repair to the familiar camaraderie of the Mess. It felt a bit strange in the evening to start with, but the glamour of arriving back at one's very own home to be greeted by Barbara was pure delight. Nevertheless, something had to be done to get us organized for this new, strange life.

So we bought Benjamin Benz for thirty pounds from an officer who was on his way home. This was a 1936 Mercedes ex-taxi of uncertain fitness and large capacity. It brought the element of adventure back into Barbara's life in more ways than one, once she had passed the obligatory test on German traffic laws. The second measure was to arrive home one sports afternoon with a small alsatian puppy stuffed inside my rugby shirt. He was an outstanding success, and we called him Syn because we had just read *Dr Syn* by Russell Thorndike. Meanwhile Peter and Jill saw to it that we entered quickly into the lively social life of the garrison, and we thought we were getting settled.

Lieutenant Colonel Tony Lascelles had other ideas. The life of an Adjutant is stimulating as the Colonel's personal staff officer. There can be no better way for a young man to learn and understand how a regiment ticks. There is much responsibility, notably for discipline, and also for translating a good deal of the Colonel's wishes into reality. There is much to learn here about diplomacy. In my case I was dealing with senior majors who had real war experience. So did the RSM, and the Chief Clerk in my Orderly Room. Most importantly, an Adjutant had to be readily accessible and usually worked longer hours than most. What the Colonel noted was that Beardsworth was high-tailing off to Gremmendorf sharp at five every afternoon.

'If I am to endure a married adjutant,' he declared, 'I must have him living close by.'

The outcome of this pronouncement was the application of a severe armlock on the garrison married quarter organization. Effectively, I was awarded an amazing number of points, with the result that we took over the major's quarter that was closest to the regiment, just in time to celebrate Halloween. We had been in Gremmendorf for just two months, and now we were within walking distance of the Officers' Mess.

Number 63 Rumphorstweg was a revelation to us, and very good for morale. We were to enjoy a four-bedroomed house with two big reception rooms that could be turned into one, and a living-in help. There was a large cellar and a large attic. The cellar contained a boiler which was serviced for us, and there was lots of room for Syn. It was one of the finest quarters we ever lived in. We were very lucky newly-weds.

One of the spin-offs from National Service was the wide span of talent among the young men who came to us for the compulsory period of two years. This included sport, and the Colonel made no bones about advertising the Sixth as a home for boxers and athletes. We had an exceptional boxing team, including two Amateur Boxing Association champions, and an athletics team that swept all before it in the British Army of the Rhine.

I owned up to my previous experience in the First as a very bad hurdler. Sadly, I was never able to clear all ten hurdles with three strides in between, and had to change down to five strides before I got to the end. In spite of this, I was allowed to join the hurdling team of four, there being nobody else foolish enough to attempt it. At least I could provide entertainment for the spectators as I ploughed my way down the course. By this means I earned the privilege of enjoying our many successes in the athletics arena. Our relay teams were a joy to watch, and we excelled in all the field events as well. In due course, we came to Aldershot as BAOR champions for the Army Finals and acquitted ourselves well.

There was an occasion when, with the help of Benjamin Benz, I was taking my now pregnant wife plus the hammer-throwing team to Hannover for a competition. We began to run out of petrol on the autobahn, but I reassured my passengers that Benjamin Benz had a solution to that one, and I proudly switched over to a reserve tank. The inevitable happened, and we drifted to a halt in the emergency lane some ten miles short of the next filling station. This was a serious matter, and the hammer-throwing team began to swell their chests at me. To our great amazement, however, the driver of an enormous pantechnicon saw our plight and stopped. Out came some fragile-looking furniture tape and a tow rope was fashioned. It was no surprise to us when it snapped as our new friend moved off. Nothing daunted, he doubled up the tape to make a shorter tow rope that could not have been more than twelve feet long.

There followed one of the most terrifying experiences of our young lives. We moved off successfully the second time and gathered speed. Benjamin Benz had never, ever been so fast. Every rivet vibrated. I hung on to the shuddering steering wheel, and Barbara hung on to the hammer-throwers, as we roared along behind the cliff in front of us and actually overtook a Volkswagen. We entered a time warp, with my foot steadily pumping the brake lest the fiend in front were to brake suddenly. To give him his due, he braked very carefully for the last half mile before we were delivered in a state of shock to the filling station. Somehow, Barbara had managed not to give birth, and Benjamin Benz had hung together. We bought a bottle of hock for our smiling, gung-ho samaritan and made the competition in time.

As for boxing, I remained firmly in the spectator seats – until the Colonel decreed that there would be an inter-squadron fiesta at every weight, and that the Adjutant was not excused. To Barbara's dismay I won my first bout, more by good luck than anything. Then I came up against an orderly room clerk with a medical grading lower than the norm for the Royal Armoured Corps. Sadly, this had no effect upon his excellent straight left and, in spite of much urgent coaching from the Sergeant-Major, I failed to defend myself. I am told the referee (a friendly and understanding padre) stopped the fight. I woke up climbing the stairs in the Officers' Mess, where they rescued me, gave me a beer, and ultimately restored me to the arms of a solicitous but angry wife.

After a few months, Colonel Tony handed over the regiment to Lieutenant Colonel Tom Gibbon. Here was another warrior from the War, whose right arm had been shot off at the shoulder during the desert battles in North Africa. He wore a false arm that could bend at the elbow and twist at the wrist, and the hand had a spring-loaded thumb. His was a splendidly calm and strong character, with a presence that carried off his somewhat piratical appearance with great élan. He put me on probation as his Adjutant, and in due course allowed me to continue in the post.

I can still feel the weight of his false arm descending onto my shoulder when he came into the office to find out what I was up to. And there were the occasions when we were partners at bridge during regimental training periods under canvas on Luneberg Heath. Colonel Tom would arrange his cards in a fan under his spring-loaded thumb before bidding commenced. I was dummy one evening and, without thinking, asked if I could see his hand.

'Of course,' he said, untwisting his false hand and passing the entire contraption across the table to me, cards and all. It was this kind of thing that speedily removed any kind of awkwardness people might have felt over his disability.

In fact, the Colonel wore out an arm about every six months, and there was a time when he asked the LAD to carry out some repair work. A day or two later he came to the office in high good humour. That morning he had put on the repaired arm for the first time, minus hand, and prepared to slot in his nail brush attachment. To do this, he would sort of shrug his right shoulder to cause the arm to bend at the elbow, and the forearm part would settle in horizontal mode. Unfortunately, the LAD had assembled the arm incorrectly, and when the Colonel did his little shrug, the arm shot out sideways instead of forwards, no doubt causing many loud guffaws to emerge from the bathroom. I enjoyed my next task of summoning the LAD commander to explain himself.

* * *

The opportunity came for a spell of leave and, in spite of Barbara's advanced pregnancy, we decided to spend the bulk of it under canvas. We gave Benjamin Benz a critical once-over, and convinced ourselves that, apart from a leaky radiator, he was fit enough to take us to Interlaken and back. There was bags of cargo space, so we were able to load up a rather bulky tank bivouac, plus a twenty-litre jerrican of water to take care of the radiator. Another unique item of equipment was a field cooker which used petrol as fuel. Every tank had one, and it needed a combination of genius and tolerance to make it work. So we needed an extra petrol can, which was just as well after our experience with the hammer-throwers.

At about that time there was a young couple in the regiment who had married sinfully below the age of twenty-five, and the rest of us marrieds were busy passing them from attic to attic until they could qualify for a quarter. We gave them our house for the period of our holiday and off we went.

The first leg as far as Bonn showed us that the radiator problem was more serious than we had imagined. We stayed in a boarding house, and visited a garage in the morning. We were given a powder called P3 to put in the radiator, on the assurance that all would now be well. The consequence was that we frothed our way up the Mosel river and over the mountains of the Vosges, attracting much attention among the locals. We got to Strasbourg safely after two days, bought a can-opener as our only souvenir, and stayed at another boarding house. On the way, our petrol cooker had gone into a sulk and never recovered.

The next day we arrived in the vicinity of the Black Forest, where I suggested to Barbara that she should map-read us into Freiburg. After a while we began to climb a steep hill, and found ourselves passing prominent kilometre signs telling us how far we had gone. It took us forty-five minutes to climb one of the highest motorcycle hill climbs in Europe, a mountain known as the Feldberg. We stopped frequently to refill the radiator as Benjamin Benz gasped his way to the top. We were nowhere near Freiburg and the view from the top was rather disappointing. So we came down again, this time taking only ten minutes, and made camp.

In the morning, we had a flat tyre, no water, no petrol, no oil, a burnt-out coil - and it was raining. A passing motorcyclist helped us to achieve rescue, and by midday we were restored to a semblance of order. Unusual measures were called for to put us properly on an even keel, and when we got to Basle we telephoned the home of a Swiss armoured regimental commander. After completing a formal visit to the Sixth some months earlier, he had most generously offered an open invitation to call upon him. His wife answered our call, and her welcome was most gracious, speaking in perfect idiomatic English.

We decided to have an omelette before arriving at the house, not knowing how meals would pan out. It was just as well, for we had to wait until breakfast the following morning, when we murdered some toast and cheese. This was no fault of our generous hosts. It was simply that, in Barbara's case, being now seven months pregnant, she retired exhausted to bed. Meanwhile, the Colonel had been run to earth by his wife in a hotel somewhere, and after welcoming me over the telephone, I was invited to join him. In due course a glamorous young woman turned up to fetch me in a Ferrari and accelerated me away for what was to become a very lengthy evening - without food.

Apparently the Colonel was the chairman of a major motoring organization which had been sponsoring a rally, and we were now to have a party. It was no surprise to me that the Ferrari driver had won the women's section. Unsurprisingly, she excused herself before we arrived at some night club, where we propped up the bar until the small hours. An abiding memory is of the moment when the Colonel's son leant towards me conspiratorially and said, 'Always when my father is not looking, I am making ze joke with ze barmaid.'

Not ten minutes later, the Colonel breathed in my ear, 'Always when my son is not looking, I am making ze joke with ze barmaid.'

Somehow I struggled out of bed the following morning, and we set off on the last lap to Interlaken, which our hosts had spoken of as 'the sink of Switzerland'. This was not to imply sleaze, only rain. And it was thus. Our only glimpse of the magnificent trio of Mönch, Eiger and Jungfrau came during our first evening as we frothed and banged towards our campsite at the foot of the Jungfrau. For the next four days there was perpetual mist and rain.

It became clear that our experiences at the Feldberg had ruined our budget. The money needed for fuel, oil and cigarettes meant that we were reduced to living on bread and oranges. Our nearest source of money (and cigarettes) was Köln (Cologne), and we decided to return northwards with a week of our holiday still to go. For some reason we were unable to alert the young couple staying in our house, and literally surprised them on the doorstep. What followed was a major challenge to everybody's good manners, but we were restored to our own bedroom, and joined the party which had been arranged for that evening. It was an odd ending to an eventful holiday.

Family life began with the arrival of Jonathan in mid-August of 1955. At the same time we were preparing for a regimental move to Tidworth at the end of the year. But things did not go to plan. That autumn Barbara went down with pleurisy, for which the cause was diagnosed as tuberculosis. This must have come from Barbara's regular visits to the sad cantonments of Displaced Persons housed in one of the barracks in Munster. All the army wives used to do this, bringing small gifts and some comfort to all manner of people from every walk of life.

So Barbara went into the British Military Hospital at about the time the regiment left for Tidworth. For my part, I took Jonathan home to my mother-in-law at Beaminster, with the help of our German maid. Then I returned to Munster to receive a warm welcome from the officers of the 14th/20th King's Hussars, with whom it was agreed I should have temporary lodging. They had taken over our barracks and equipment from us and were settling down to a tour of some years with BAOR. They introduced me to 'The Emperor', a marvellous solid silver chamber pot captured during the Napoleonic wars. It was always filled (appropriately) with champagne during big dinner nights, finishing upside down over the head of the youngest cornet.

In February, Barbara was given a clean bill of health, or so we thought. We flew home in a medical Dakota and staged at Tidworth Military Hospital. Our new doctor exposed the brutal fact that Barbara had completed only two months in hospital, and there would be four more to come. That was a real shaker. I installed Barbara at the Army Chest Hospital near Hindhead, and my mother-in-law continued to look after Jonathan, now six months old.

The Colonel posted me across into A Squadron as second-in-command. I began a routine of visiting Barbara at weekends and Jonathan rather less often. There was no doubt that Barbara needed the long, graduated convalescence imposed upon her. There were lots of fellow patients, including a remarkable contingent of Gurkhas. The wonder drug was streptomycin, and it is worth a note that the Army Chest Hospital closed not long after Barbara's eventual departure.

Back with the Sixth, I returned to mess life, and enjoyed meeting old friends from the First who, coincidentally, were also stationed in Tidworth. Then came an assignment as Technical Adjutant of a temporary summer camp at Tilshead in the centre of Salisbury Plain. A Squadron from the First and A Squadron from the Sixth were to join forces and supply territorial regiments of the Royal Armoured Corps with tanks and vehicles for their annual training. My job was to account for all the bits and pieces of equipment - including tanks - and to be responsible for their availability.

I was enjoying myself at Tilshead, but Barbara was not enjoying her hospital ward, and we longed for a return to family life.

CHAPTER VI

SUEZ

It is a savage irony that, the very day I got Barbara back home to her parents and her son at Meerhay Manor, the Suez crisis broke over our heads. We had not even got as far as the front door before my mother-in-law burst out into the garden with a stricken expression. She gave us an urgent message from the regiment to say that I should report back for duty the next day. At least we had one night of family solidarity.

From that moment we had some three weeks to paint everything in sight a dull desert yellow, and also get in some urgent gunnery practice on Larkhill ranges. But first we had to clear up the territorial camp and, as Technical Adjutant, I was a touch nervous. Imagine my delight when we were told that a national emergency changed the rules. All we had to do was throw back into store anything we could find, whether or not it was in good working order. This was quite unheard of. The men at the depot in Ludgershall who took back all our vehicles and equipment, not to mention some highly priced tanks, simply scrawled chalk marks on everything like satisfied customs officers. I suspect the only ones who were genuinely unhappy about this method of accounting were those who had to don green eyeshades and sort out the mess in the Treasury.

Life took on a hectic pace in both the First and the Sixth, for both regiments were under orders for Suez. The Colonel ran a conference every evening at 1800 hours to check on progress, and the business of preparation went on regardless of night or day. The regiment had to be brought up to war establishment, which meant that our manpower increased by about half as much again. I remember that the establishment for A Squadron was just over 150, including reserve crews, officers' mess staff, a larger echelon of soft-skinned vehicles with their drivers and cooks, and a bigger Light Aid Detachment (LAD) of REME.

There were to be forty-eight heavy armoured fighting vehicles (AFVs) including three armoured recovery vehicles (ARVs). RHQ had three command tanks with a special radio fit, and each squadron had two control tanks in SHQ, also with a different radio fit, and four troops of three tanks.

All this meant that new tanks and vehicles had to be taken on charge, inspected, worked on and painted. Our existing fleet received the same treatment, and modification and repair went on at all hours on a shift basis. Meanwhile, a proclamation had been issued for the call-up of reservists, and they began to arrive in numbers to make up our establishment.

The reservists were excellent and served as a much-needed leavening among our younger regulars, some of whom had only just learnt their first trade. The difference was that the reservists had been out in the wild and woolly world after their National Service, and had come back with a maturity of outlook that was most refreshing. Many of them had three trades to their name, and by their presence contributed significantly to our professionalism and efficiency. Among the officers there was an academic type who had been a civilian for ten years. At the other end of the scale there was an old friend who had only just left us a few months previously after completing a short-service commission. Most reservists, though, had been in civilian life for two to three years.

It was about this time that we learnt Buchanan's Law. Duncan Buchanan was a New Zealander with a regular commission in the British Army, and it was our good fortune to have him with us in A Squadron as the senior troop leader. He was driving me towards Bulford one day in my Rover when the Divisional Commander came past in the other direction, sporting his two-star plate on the bumper. I saluted, whereupon Duncan began by wondering whether he should have taken his hands off the wheel and saluted as well. His Law evolved, which was to the effect that, in normal circumstances, the number of salutes offered should equal the number of stars on the senior officer's car. However, there was an exception if a Field Marshal was seen approaching with five stars, whereupon we should stop the Rover, switch off, get out, clamber onto the roof and wave.

We soon got to hear that the First would be moving south for embarkation, and that they would set sail before the Sixth, who would be going to Plymouth. The buzz of expectation increased, and a plan was evolved to get everyone a 48-hour pass before it was too late. It was good to disappear down to Beaminster to discover Barbara on the slow road to recovery, albeit rather frail in comparison with her normal vigorous self. Coincidentally, our regimental Recce Troop were in the area on a movement and signals exercise and, by arrangement, they came to tackle the very steep hill climb behind Meerhay Manor that brought them out on top of Beaminster Down. Naturally, we gave them an administrative break. And all of them got up the hill.

It was about this time that misfortune struck the First. Maritime logistics had gone wrong somewhere and the First could not embark. To their intense annoyance and our delight, the Sixth were put first in the order of march on the way to Malta.

Very soon, the movement to Plymouth began and B Squadron would be the pathfinders, with orders to sail several days before the rest of us. There was to be a military fleet of tank transporters manned by reservists, but since the mobilization of their unit was incomplete, B Squadron had to rely on the civilian market. A well-known company was hired for the job, and things got under way.

It was agonizingly slow. The make of transporter was of the kind that had to have the whole of the back axle removed before the tank could be coaxed on board. That, and various other union rules, decreed that any sort of urgency flew out of the window, and the usual turn-round time to Plymouth and back turned out to be three days. There was worse to come. At 1700 hours on the Friday, the foreman in charge at Tidworth called a halt for the weekend, in mid-load as it were. The interview that followed in the Colonel's office was a little tense.

'Do you not realize,' said the Colonel, 'that there is a national emergency?'

'I dunno about that, Guv,' replied the foreman. 'Rules is rules and we'll start again sharp Monday morning.'

There was no shifting this position by anyone higher up the chain of command, and the Colonel remained incandescent. It did not help matters when we heard tell of a transporter driver who stopped in a lay-by en route to Plymouth on the same Friday. The lay-by was close to a convenient hostelry, where the driver spent the weekend, leaving the tank outside, fully 'bombed up' with live ammunition. The turn-round time for that guy was five days.

By the time B Squadron had got themselves to Plymouth, the reservist transporter squadron appeared on the scene at Tidworth to shouts of welcome. They began to load up the rest of us at normal speed, and turn-round time for them was twenty-four hours. Much better!

Our few days at Plymouth were bitter sweet, in the tradition of all romantic novels. A part of this was due to our New Zealander, Duncan Buchanan. We learnt that, three years before in New Zealand, he and his sweetheart Mary had declared their love for each other. Now, after all this time, she was on board a boat for Liverpool, where she would arrive a couple of days before we were due to set sail ourselves. A very nervous officer was despatched to Liverpool with cries of encouragement and solidarity from the rest of us. Would it be OK, or would everything turn to worms? We need not have worried. The blissful couple appeared in Plymouth with wide grins, and yet another party began. They were married when we returned from Egypt, and lived happily ever after.

Quite a lot of girls came to Plymouth to see us off, including Barbara. We made whoopee in the Octagon Restaurant on our last night, when I fear a few bread rolls took to the air. And then we had to say goodbye and get going.

From the total of 48 AFVs, 45 went to sea and 3 were left 'dead' on the quayside. From that moment, all the tanks and ARVs remained fit, in spite of being cooped up for long periods aboard ship, and very little movement on land. Tanks are like horses and prefer to be out and about. The only snag which cropped up turned out to be a generic fuel problem that affected engines starting in the hot weather. Fortunately, some experts from a major oil company sorted that out for us in Malta.

I suppose it took us some ten days to reach the George Cross island. The bulk of A Squadron went aboard HMS *Ravager*, one of the LSTs (Landing Ship Tank) manned by the Royal Navy. We took eleven Centurion tanks (two in SHQ and three troops of three) plus the ARV, which had to board last because of its shape. This meant, of course, that it would be first out! Our Ferret scout cars and the soft-skinned vehicles went with us on the top deck, and the fourth troop went in a composite party with RHQ in another LST.

To stow the tanks, it was important first of all to reverse carefully through the bow doors until the rear road wheels started to climb a large wooden sleeper placed in the correct position. A second sleeper was rammed under the front road wheels before the driver let off the brake to allow the tank to slide forward an inch or two, settling snugly on its tracks between the two sleepers. Then we used very powerful naval jacks to raise the tank hull onto heavy wooden blocks, thus taking the weight off the suspension. Finally, four big chains connected the tank towing hooks to 'elephant's feet' located in the tank deck floor, two chains at each end crossing each other in the form of an X. When these chains were tightened up, the tank was thought ready to face the Bay of Biscay.

I was not ready for the Bay of Biscay. I think I have explained that I am not a good sailor. A flat-bottomed LST with a blunt bow has an appalling motion, particularly when the sea is beam on. I made it quite clear that, if anyone wanted my advice or a decision, they should come to see me in my cabin. It seemed to me that I would be useless to anyone if I tried to provide moral encouragement to the stalwart souls who visited the surging tank deck to check on the tightness of the chains. The Navy were rather keen that no tank should work loose in the hold, and this was an important duty.

However, when anyone did come to my cabin, they found me in uniform and free from nausea. My technique was to take three seasick tablets daily. I rose, washed, shaved and dressed every morning, and ate breakfast in the wardroom. I could get back to my bunk just in time to fight off the nausea. Lunch was the most difficult. But provided I lay down, this wimpish officer maintained a military capability of sorts.

Things got better off the coast of Spain, and I found with many others that a pitching motion could be endured up on deck without difficulty. When we rounded Gibraltar and began to head eastwards, a holiday spirit emerged. Dolphins gambolled in the bow wave, creating beautiful streaks of phosphorescence in the gloaming. But we also had PT sessions in the warm sun, and got down to a programme of training and operational briefings.

For my part, it was good to soak up the naval atmosphere, which I suppose was deep in my psyche. I enjoyed the way Number One responded to the Captain with 'aye-aye, sir', and the problems of navigation, and the way the watches were organized on the bridge. Entry to the bridge was not to be assumed. A polite request from halfway up the ladder was de rigueur for us pongos, but a warm welcome always followed.

The view from the bridge taught us much about the design of the LST, which had to flex an astonishing amount to avoid breaking up altogether. If the Captain allowed too many engine revolutions against a head-on sea, the effect of the blunt bow crashing into a big wave could be dramatic. But even when the balance was right, the flexing of the long forward deck was always remarkable. There were six three-ton ammunition or petrol trucks secured on deck, three in line-ahead to port and to starboard of the central cover over the inboard ramp. In a heavy sea, the centre truck of three could be seen to be either above or below the others as the deck beneath them flexed.

We had the inescapable desire to tell the Captain about it, and of course we did, and there began the first lesson.

Entry into Grand Harbour at Valetta provided further education. 'Dress ship for entry into harbour' meant just that, and one must *not* open an entry port onto the main deck, as I did, a minute or so after the Master-at-Arms has shut it. To keep us out of further trouble, my squadron leader Robin Grierson and I were permitted on the bridge where we could be kept under surveillance, provided we remained precisely where we were put, and adopted the formal 'stand-at-ease' position. This gave us a grandstand view of the marvellously impressive harbour that I remembered from twenty years back.

The exchange of salutations between warships is hallowed by time, and in this case always had to be initiated by HMS *Ravager*, an LST being the most junior form of life imaginable in the Royal Navy, apart from midshipmen. This was particularly evident in the languid demeanour of our first customer, the Officer-of-the-Watch in a beautiful gleaming cruiser, telescope under arm, as he eyed us from the quarterdeck. Number One gave an order and saluted, an able seaman next to him blew his pipes, and a yeoman in the stern lowered our ensign. An immaculate response came back from the cruiser, the sound of the pipes wafting across the bright dappled water of the outer harbour, and their ensign dipped in reply. The Captain ignored all this and, from the topmost part of the bridge, concentrated on driving his ship to its berth.

There were many more ships of the fleet in harbour that day to receive our greeting, all of it conducted with élan. However, there were two further compulsory salutes which had to be directed at inanimate cliff faces, and these made our naval friends nervous. One was for Fort St Angelo where my father had once worked, and the other was for a NATO Headquarters below Barracca Gardens. Behind each cliff, we were told, stood an irascible admiral with a telescope who would be quite capable of telling us to go back and do the whole thing again. We drifted by without any Nelson-type signals, and heaved sighs of relief.

Malta was not designed to take tanks, and there was not much room for us either. Our home was to be the sporting complex at the far end of Grand Harbour known as the Marsa. Our tents and marquees went up in the centre of the athletic track and, to the great dismay of some of our hosts, we drove our tanks onto the reserve polo ground. It was quite a hard, dusty piece of ground which, as it happened, suffered little damage from the tanks because of the relatively low ground pressure under the tracks. On the other hand, the heavy ammunition and petrol trucks gouged out great ruts in the surface, and the worst fears of the resident polo players were confirmed. In spite of this felony, the officers were graciously offered honorary membership of the Polo Club, which turned out to be a great boon.

There was no certainty that we would be going to war, but we trained as best as we could in expectation of it. The principal decision was to 'waterproof' all the tanks of C Squadron so that they could wade ashore immediately behind, and in support of, a commando assault over the beaches. Waterproofing kit was cumbersome and unsightly but nonetheless effective. Its purpose was to allow a tank to wade up to a depth which brought the surface of the sea up to a point above the turret ring, which is the interface between turret and hull. Thus a means had to be found to prevent sea water leaking through the turret ring, which would have upset the driver, or leaking into the engine compartment, which would have upset everybody. It took a long time to fit the equipment or dismantle it manually, but after operational use it could be blown off on the beach using an explosive charge.

Because of their operational role, C Squadron were dispersed among a fleet of LCTs (Landing Craft Tank) as opposed to the rest of us in LSTs. An LCT accommodated one troop of tanks only.

The Navy had plenty of training of their own to do, and several times over the next couple of months we practised getting our vehicles and tanks aboard as fast as possible, and unloading again. While the loading of a tank was hard work, the loading of a very heavily laden ammunition truck was distinctly hairy. The inboard ramp in an LST, which permitted access from the tank deck to the top deck, had two major disadvantages. First, it had no kerb at the sides to collect a wheel that was going off line. Secondly, at the point where vehicles emerged onto the top deck, there was a horrid bump created by the massive hinges of the ramp. My role was to stand a pace back from the top of the ramp and direct the drivers as they tackled the steep incline, hopefully without slipping the clutch in panic. The moment of panic was always likely to be at the top of the ramp when, because of the bump, the front wheels rose over it and the drivers could no longer see any part of me except my forearms held high above my head.

One driver of an ammunition truck did panic, going over the bump. He slipped his clutch, and we watched with our hearts in our mouths as I sought to keep him straight while he rolled slowly backwards on his brakes to the foot of the ramp. After he did it a second time, he was turfed out of his truck by a sweating NCO, who took his place and showed how it should be done.

We devised signals and map-reading exercises which took the commanders all over the island in Ferrets and rover vehicles. The difficult map-reading occurred within the small towns and villages, where it became all too common for us to emerge into the open going in completely the wrong direction. This was because of the extremely narrow, twisting streets in which it was easy to lose one's sense of direction, particularly when it came to a fork in the road. All this gave us plenty of practice, as well as the opportunity to relish the harsh yellow-cum-olive landscape and the brilliant blue of sea and sky. Every settlement seemed to be dominated by a large domed or towered church, and the fields in between were positively tiny.

We had to stay fit and my squadron leader decreed a forced march on one occasion. He asked me, with my local knowledge, where we might go, and I immediately thought of Peter's Pool, south-east along the coast from Grand Harbour. I had learnt to swim there, and it was very beautiful and quite secluded. So our route was planned and off we went.

When we finally descended the path to Peter's Pool, four beautiful Wrens were stretched out enjoying some uninterrupted sunbathing, or so they thought. The impact upon them of 150 sweating tankies was significant, and the impact of them upon our troopers was worse. There followed all manner of macho displays as the men launched themselves noisily off the rocks into the perfect translucent water, which a while earlier had been lapping gently to the shore in every shade of green and blue.

The Wrens became extremely angry, and I am afraid departed rather quickly in their dashing red sports car, leaving our social image in some disarray.

While we regretted this incident, we need not have worried about our social image. We became extremely popular, because we seemed to provide a sort of no man's land where rival social circles in Malta could actually meet and talk to each other. To begin with, when not involved in training, our daily routine started very early in the morning and finished around 1400 hours or so. It became a habit to organize swimming parties of various kinds, and a number of the officers had responded readily to an open invitation from the Royal Marine headquarters in St George's Bay to use a sort of lido they had set up, with rafts out in the bay and so forth.

One of the reservist officers in C Squadron was a member of the Royal Ocean Racing Club, and had met a fellow sailing enthusiast who was a Lieutenant Commander in the NATO headquarters. Naturally enough, this naval officer and his wife joined us at the lido for a swim one afternoon. We were totally astonished to hear his wife remark wistfully that this was the first time in the eighteen months since their posting began in Malta that they had come swimming in St George's Bay.

'Oh, but this is just for the Marines, you see,' she said. 'Thank you so much for having us!'

In this way we began to learn that the naval, marine, army and air force coteries hardly ever mixed, in spite of living cheek by jowl in one small island. We threw several parties in our marquee on the Marsa, which were a tremendous success with our guests falling upon each other in delight at being able to meet somebody new. It was nice to feel wanted.

There was just one occasion when we created some excitement by moving our tanks across the island to Ghain Tuffieha in order to train with the Marines. The move was conducted at night, and the actual training was extraordinarily limited because of the fiendishly rocky track which our tanks had to use without any opportunity for manoeuvre. But it was very hard work for the Marines, who were required by their commanders to gallop along in the considerable heat wearing gas masks. We, on the other hand, lounged in the security of our tank turrets with a mug of tea to hand. Indeed, it is this ability to produce hot refreshment from within our tanks to all who need it that makes us so popular with our long-suffering infantry friends.

After some weeks, four of us in A Squadron decided to bring our wives out to Malta, and in my case Jonathan too, aged eleven months. The others were Robin Grierson, Squadron Sergeant-Major Carse and Staff Sergeant Durbidge of REME who ran our LAD section. I have no recollection of quite why we were the only ones to do this, but it was an excellent move as far as I was concerned.

I knew Jonathan had arrived from the noise he was making after the steep descent to Luqa airport in, as the Americans would say, a rinky-dink airline from London. Barbara and I took him to the Plevna Court Hotel in Sliema, and there we settled in. It was great to be able to show Barbara the sights. There was my old home in Dockyard Creek, the beaches at Ghain Tuffieha, St Paul's Bay and Mellieha Bay towards the north of the island, and a look across to Gozo. The churches were magnificent, and the deep tolling of the bells a fitting reminder of normality. The great promontory carrying Floriana and Valetta itself is a unique sight, with marvellous views of warships and commercial liners spread throughout Grand Harbour and Sliema Bay.

The Suez crisis began to hot up a bit, and we were visited by our operational commander, Lieutenant General Sir Hugh Stockwell, who had been commandant at Sandhurst when I was there as a cadet. We still thought at this time that Alexandria would be our most likely destination. But all General Hughie would say was that we were 'due for a duffy in Egypt'.

We were also visited by a senior correspondent of the *Daily Mail*, whose approach to things was odd to say the least. Suffice to say that the article which appeared in the paper a few days later was greeted with derision among the troops.

Then we conducted another loading-up exercise, but this time there was an undercurrent. Sure enough, when all the tanks and vehicles were aboard, we were told that 'this was it', and I barely had time to tell Barbara before we were off.

Barbara and Joan Grierson eventually got themselves on the same plane to Nice where, for some reason, they had to remain overnight. The French treated them with great gallic élan, being virtually comrades-in-arms, as it were.

'*Voilà les pauvres femmes anglaises! Leurs maris sont parti à la guerre! Oh la! la!*'

They were housed in the finest suites in a grand four-star hotel, free of charge. Barbara's father was in London to greet her when she finally arrived with Jonathan, to be told that there had been a ceasefire.

We formed convoy outside Grand Harbour, and immediately the rot set in. There was an unpleasant swell, to say the least. In these conditions Robin Grierson summoned us to his cabin for an O Group, and the ceremonial opening of sealed orders. We got as far as realizing that Port Said was to be our goal and then, one by one, we excused ourselves sheepishly and tottered to our cabins for a lie-down. Robin was left on his own, wondering whether he had an operational squadron or not.

All was well again within twenty-four hours, and we began to concentrate on our orders and ponder upon events. We had plenty of time, for the speed of our convoy was controlled by the best speed of the small LCTs, which was something like seven to nine knots, depending upon the swell.

Fresh air photos were delivered to us by airdrop, and we began detailed planning. There was a time when the Colonel was brought round by barge to issue his final orders to squadron commanders and to speak to the men. We also had a small party of marines on board who had a mission of their own, and who would be leaving us for the beaches long before we made our landfall. They spent many hours in a huddle, going through their plans over and over again.

For us, there was lots of PT, checking of stowage and cleaning of equipment. And we began to feel nervous. For most of us, this was the first time we were going to have to do what we were paid and trained for. We were preparing, in A Squadron, for an expected confrontation with enemy armour coming from Cairo to meet us. There would be a tank battle if that happened, so we rehearsed and rehearsed our turret drills

Landing Ship Tank (LST) leaving Grand Harbour, Valetta, 1956

and fire orders.

Among the officers, I remember leaning over the rail on a particularly lovely evening when we discussed what it was that we were doing. The political scenario coming through to us was far from cut and dried, and while we were there to obey orders, it was useful to find one's own inner conviction. It was different, I think, for all of us. My own clear vision was that we were doing what the French and ourselves felt the UN should be doing, and since they had done nothing but talk, here we were. In the end the simple motivation for everybody, including the soldiers, was that we were there to 'teach Nasser a lesson'. And all the time we were shadowed by the US Sixth Fleet.

We learnt that all the official communications for the coming operation had to be in ZULU time (GMT), although the local sun time was BRAVO, and we were actually setting our watches to CHARLIE time, or local summer time, you might say. This sounds confusing, and it was to start with. But it made sense to operate on local summer time, as we do every year in UK, and the timings of our assault were adjusted accordingly. Whereas the Commander-in-Chief and all at home needed to relate all activity to GMT, or so they said.

When dawn broke on 6 November 1956, we could see from our station, a mile or two offshore, the palls of smoke rising from the burning buildings of Port Said and the adjacent airfield. The Paras had landed the day before, and the Marines were launching themselves over the beach, with C Squadron in support. There was much air activity.

The confusion in Port Said was considerable, with the civilian population everywhere intermingled and often indistinguishable from army elements offering resistance. This caused difficulty for some young tank gunners when, for example, the Commandos wanted a machine-gun in a first-floor balcony eliminated by a supporting tank. One troop sergeant earned an award for his leadership in these difficult circumstances.

Meanwhile HMS *Ravager*, with the bulk of A Squadron on board, steamed slowly towards the mouth of the Suez Canal, and then turned south into it towards the harbour, following behind the minesweeper fleet. In due course it became possible to effect a landing over the quay and, with our redoubtable ARV crew leading the way, we began to come ashore. The ARV had an immediate task, which was to batter a way through the high steel fence surrounding the quayside. The rest of us then passed them by in the order troop-SHQ-troop-troop, the leading troop leader being Duncan Buchanan. The fourth troop, of course, would have to join later when the composite party with RHQ made it ashore.

We motored without delay round the harbour perimeter, avoiding the fighting in the town itself. Only the odd stray rifle bullet came in our direction, leaving a couple of dents in the tool bins surrounding the turret. The general scene was mostly of bloated corpses of horses and donkeys and goats that had suffered in the air strikes. Eventually, in the southern outskirts, the opportunity came to deploy across a railway track onto a golf course, which was no more than a hard sandy expanse of relatively smooth ground.

What followed was a severe embarrassment. Sergeant Jachnik of the leading troop became bogged, for the hard ground was less resilient than we had imagined, and the tracks broke through the surface to make the tank immobile. Buchanan tried to tow him out, and got bogged himself. The troop corporal tried to tow his troop leader out, and was the third to get bogged. Finally, like a fool, I thought I could get the corporal out, and my tank was the fourth to succumb. One could say it was misplaced enthusiasm, allied to a wish not to have anyone caught defenceless by a man with a bazooka.

What actually happened was that one of our own aircraft came over and decided to attack Sergeant Jachnik. This was in spite of a large white H painted onto every vehicle roof to aid identification. Call it the fog of war, the result of which was a cannon shell lodged in the armour next to the petrol tank. No conflagration occurred, and Jachnik and his crew got away with it.

Once again the ARV crew came into their own. They took up station on the railway track that bordered the golf course, giving them a very secure base for the recovery that followed. Using a series of linked tow ropes, all four tanks were recovered in the course of the next few hours.

Fortunately there was a pause before the next phase of operations. A Squadron were expecting to be ordered south on the main road to El Qantara, a town some sixty miles distant which we needed to reach before we could deploy off the road. As it happened, our ignominious experience on the golf course had not held things up.

The terrain southward from Port Said needs some explanation. There were in fact two roads running parallel with the Suez Canal which we needed to use for our advance. Immediately west of the Canal was the so-called Canal Road, which was fairly narrow and bounded on its west side by another waterway known as the Sweet Water Canal. West again came the railway, and west of that many acres of wetlands lying between the railway and the main road south which would carry the bulk of our force. West again were literally square miles of lagoons running southward. Thus the tanks which we deployed on the Canal Road would be quite isolated from the rest of us, squeezed in between the Sweet Water Canal and the Suez Canal itself. Moreover, nobody could get off either road before reaching El Qantara, except to park temporarily on a wider area of hard ground at each of the small railway stations en route to El Qantara. There were three of these, and the southernmost was called El Cap.

It was dark before we were launched. I recall the feeling of security we felt in SHQ to have four soldiers from the French Foreign Legion with us, two on the back decks of each tank. This was mainly because, during a short halt, Buchanan had walked away to answer a call of nature and, on his return, found himself looking down the barrel of a legionnaire's gun. Buchanan raised his arms high above his head and explained his friendly nature.

'*Venez*,' said the Frenchman quietly, pointing his gun straight between Duncan's eyes. He was allowed to pass, and from that moment we felt secure.

The Parachute Brigade Commander, Brigadier Tubby Butler, came south with us in his jeep, closely escorted by A Squadron. The aim was to get as far south as possible before the ceasefire came into effect. We travelled fast without lights, which got a bit hairy for the tank drivers and their commanders, for the main road included a number of right-angled double bends, and the water was never far away off the side of the road. However, the scene behind us was reminiscent of Blackpool *en fête* as parachute units followed us in requisitioned Egyptian trucks with all lights blazing. It was a memorable sight.

We never got to El Qantara even though, as I recall, we kept going some fifteen minutes longer than perhaps we should have done, in order to achieve at least a minimal operational position at the tiny railway station of El Cap. The scene at first light was extraordinary and thoroughly unwarlike, spread out as we were in a very long convoy line confined to the main road. There was no opportunity to deploy except for a limited force in an area of perhaps five or six acres close to the station.

Behind us, people began to sort themselves out and return to Port Said. There was one incident to distract us that morning, once again involving the redoubtable Sergeant Jachnik. His was the lead tank over to our left, out of our sight and located on the Canal Road the other side of the railway and the Sweet Water Canal. About 300 yards or so behind him was Sergeant Stebbings from a different troop giving him cover. Grierson was away at an O Group and I had the squadron.

Stebbings suddenly reported by radio that a group of the enemy, perhaps thirty strong, were creeping steadily towards Jachnik and his crew. It appeared to be a potential violation of the ceasefire. Stebbings's problem was that Jacknik was trying to sort out some trouble with his wireless, and was not responding. The driver was in the ditch on the opposite side to the approaching posse, preparing a meal, and the gunner was beside him stripping and cleaning the .30 Browning. I invited Stebbings to start up and close on Jachnik to give him warning. Stebbings demurred, saying that if he did so he would lose the clear field of fire he now had on the enemy. I ordered that Stebbings should retaliate at once if the enemy opened fire, recognizing the possible political implications if Stebbings were to take things into his own hands.

The posse did open fire, and Stebbings and his gunner set to with a will. An Egyptian bullet passed between Sergeant Jachnik's ear and his scalp, nicking him slightly. In a towering rage he dived back into his turret and emerged with a weapon at his hip to join in the fusilade. The posse retreated. We never knew the casualty list, but there were no more incidents.

The problem with officers is that they so often use their initiative with disastrous results. I was about to do just that. It was evident that we could not sit for ever on the road, and I had espied that a battery of guns had already got themselves organized with commendable efficiency in the off-road area of El Cap. I went to see if there was room for our tanks as well, and confirmed that there was. So, in my accustomed role of officer in charge of tank harbouring, I ordered the squadron into the comparative seclusion of El Cap.

What I had forgotten from my Sandhurst days is that a battery of guns depends crucially on internal communications, in this case using telephone line that had been buried an inch or so under the sand. No one noticed at first, until they ran their first practice. Then the Battery Commander went into orbit, and if my Squadron Leader and Commanding Officer had not both stood between me and him, I might not have survived to tell this tale.

After a few days there was a general withdrawal to Port Said, leaving one troop from A Squadron to man El Cap. This chore was rotated weekly. The rest of the squadron finished up in the only wood in the vicinity of Port Said, close to a waterworks where the main road debouched southwards. Close by were some of the Foreign Legion, many of whom seemed to come from Liverpool. I remember they persisted in swimming in the Sweet Water Canal, in spite of dire warnings that they would catch the dread disease bilharzia by so doing. The rest of the regiment found billets in buildings close to the beaches, and we settled down to a waiting game while the politics were sorted out. A regular recce was mounted each evening by the Recce Troop, but otherwise we confined our arrangements to protecting our perimeter.

Apart from daily conferences at RHQ, the only unusual event was our celebration of Cambrai on 20 November. Our resources were naturally limited, but we got some sport going, and found enough supplies of beer and such from the NAAFI. I decided to join my own tank crew in a lethal game known as Twenty-One Aces. Using liar dice, players take it in turns to throw, adding up the cumulative number of aces as the game proceeds. The person throwing the seventh ace nominates a drink. The person throwing the fourteenth ace pays for it. And the person throwing the twenty-first ace drinks it.

This game can get out of hand. Noting the somewhat tiddly condition of my crew, I began to wonder how best to bring things to a close. I need not have worried. It fell to me on two successive occasions to nominate the next drink. On each occasion I called for a pint of orange squash. To the unqualified delight of the rest of us, my gunner, Lance Corporal Krelle, had to drink both. I'm not sure he made it, but honour was satisfied all round.

As we moved into December, Robin Grierson had to return home to take up a posting, and I took over the squadron. By this time the United Nations troops were wanting to move into the town preparatory to our eventual departure, and so I took A Squadron to a beachside block of flats near RHQ and set up my defences. Gradually the UN force closed in on the harbour, and a phased withdrawal began. It was decreed that we should be the last squadron to leave, indeed we were probably the last sub-unit in the entire force to leave Port Said.

On our last day, 22 December, HMS *Suvla* of the Royal Navy lay at the hard with her bow doors open and all my recce and echelon vehicles stowed on her top deck. It was at this time that my mother went to the post office in Bromley with a telegram for me.

'We're so sorry, madam,' they said. 'This BFPO number has just been withdrawn, because they are pulling out of Port Said today.'

They had not reckoned with my mother's knowledge of the Senior Service, and she rang the Admiralty forthwith. A signal was beamed to Radio Malta, and passed on another frequency to HMS *Tyne*, the Admiral's flagship lying in the Canal approaches. A further message reached the Captain of HMS *Suvla*, who handed it to my squadron liaison officer, a reservist called Ian Brackenbury. He took it to our armoured ambulance on the top deck and used the squadron radio net.

I was pacing up and down in front of my tank, about half a mile away, when my sergeant operator popped his head out of the turret.

'Sir?'

'Yes?'

'Happy Christmas. God bless. Mother. SIR!'

This story gave my mother much joy. We left that evening to the accompaniment of tracer bullets shooting skyward and saluted a most enormous white ensign that had been secured to the giant flagmast by the De Lesseps statue. We celebrated Christmas and New Year at sea, calling in at Malta and Gibraltar on the way, reaching Tilbury early in January.

CHAPTER VII

LIBYA

The Sixth trickled back into Bulford Camp, the next-door garrison town to Tidworth whence our Suez adventure had begun. It was January 1957, and everyone disappeared for five weeks leave or so. It was a marvellous time for the recharging of batteries and a return to normality - or so we thought. We soon learnt that the regiment was to take over almost immediately from the Fifth Royal Tank Regiment in Libya. To be precise, we were going to a place called Barce (pronounced Barchy) in Cyrenaica, about two hours east of Benghazi. Beardsworth was to serve as the Advance Party Adjutant - move now!

But there was more to it. The longer-term plan was for me to return to Lulworth about four months later for training as the next Regimental Gunnery Officer. Exceptionally, I was to remain for an additional course on the Conqueror tank, adding to my experience of the standard Centurion. The implication of all this was that we were able to settle Barbara, Jonathan and Syn in a delightful cottage in West Lulworth below the Gunnery School, where they would await my return from Barce.

In no time at all, it seemed, I was back in North Africa, getting to know the Fifth during the short period of the handover.

Barce was up in the hill country known as the Jebel, not all that far from the beautiful Roman ruins at Cyrene on the way to Derna, and eventually Tobruk. There was a United Nations farm nearby where the corn grew as high as an elephant's eye - but nowhere else. The local farmers preferred their goats and sheep, which they liked to stable in the many houses built by Italians during the thirties. The farmers themselves saw no reason to live anywhere other than in their own tents. Barce itself was a bustling little market town, about twenty miles inland from a series of wonderful beaches. The desert was not too far away to our south, and we soon developed a fascination for it.

There was no operational role for the regiment. King Idris would not countenance a move outwards from his borders, as the Fifth had discovered during the Suez crisis. They had deployed up to the Egyptian frontier, but could go no further. We were stationed in Libya purely for the wonderful opportunity to train in the desert, without any apparent likelihood of being able to put the experience into practice.

However, given the lack of an operational role, we were placed permanently on standby to react instantly in case a civilian aircraft should crash in the desert. The scenario was that the crash would occur a maximum of three hundred miles to the south, and that at least seventy passengers and crew, alive but injured, would require rescue. As Advance Party Adjutant it was my job to understand this, and to vet the plan which had been drawn up by the Fifth. I came to the conclusion that it would be wise to add a further 3-ton truck to the convoy that had already been earmarked, on the grounds that seventy stretcher cases would need plenty of room for their exhausting journey back.

When the Colonel came out with the rest of the regiment, I put the matter to him, and he agreed with some reluctance. The dilemma was that every truck involved had to be taken off normal duty and parked in a special hangar together with its payload. Most of us felt that the disaster would never happen - but of course it *might*, and everything would then have to go like clockwork. The consequence of this decision was that there would be one less truck to take soldiers down to the beach on a late afternoon pass. Most of the time, any spare truck not earmarked for the imagined disaster would be trekking back and forth on the 160-mile round trip bringing supplies up from Benghazi.

The maps we used were to a scale of 200,000 to 1, or just over three miles to the inch. Depicting mostly desert, there was very little on them, but one crucial feature was passed on to us by the Fifth. It was the location of a so-called 'pigeon-hole' out in the desert. There were several of these, literally giant holes in the ground, that were well documented and well away from the training grounds. Typically, they would be some fifty feet across and anything up to ninety feet in depth. From time to time a party would go out in the early morning or late evening for a lively pigeon shoot around the rim of these features.

Tragically, it was a fatal accident which revealed the location of this other, distant pigeon-hole in otherwise flat and featureless desert terrain. The Fifth were engaging in some night navigation training without lights when a troop leader's tank plunged straight into it. From memory, at least one crew member was killed, and the young officer broke his back (from which he made a full recovery). A heroic rescue mission was carried out in very difficult circumstances, and the REME commander of the LAD in particular distinguished himself. In daylight, an artillery spotter plane flew over the area, and the track made by the tank in question ran as straight as a ruler for well over a mile towards the hidden, gaping hole. From that day, no training was begun without first ensuring that everybody's map was marked up to show the site of the pigeon-hole.

As the regiment settled in, we became used to the steadily increasing temperatures and the process of acclimatization. Many of the soldiers used engine oil as suntan lotion, and became very dark indeed. I was put in charge of pay, and found myself making weekly trips to the bank in Barce with a loaded revolver. Guard duty was also conducted with loaded revolvers, a practice I never encountered elsewhere except while at Port Said. The temperature climbed to sustained values over 100°F, and we needed to watch our intake of salt. It took me some time to learn the value of walking slowly.

The routine of life was rudely shattered when I learnt that I was to undergo a captain-to-major practical test, a necessary hurdle on the way up the promotion ladder. The venue was a spot just south of Tripoli, about 500 miles to the west of Barce as the crow flies. In due course, I was flown to Tripoli to join the gathering horde of young hopefuls, and we had a great time together in between the various sessions with our stern-faced examiners. To my surprise I did quite well, which was very good for brownie points when I got back to the regiment.

But then it was time to return home, after a spell of four months that had flown by.

Lulworth was a very pleasant place to be. The Gunnery School and the principal firing points look out over Arish Mel Gap and Warbarrow Bay, above and to the east of Lulworth Cove and set in the Purbeck Hills. The public have access at weekends, and can enjoy the wild, unaltered habitat that comes with the creation of a danger area. There are some who disagree with this, and protest that the range should be closed, cleared up, and built upon. The great majority of the local populace do not agree with such assertions, and cooperate willingly with the military, who bring much business.

Our own little hired cottage was called Lulcote, down the valley in the village of West Lulworth, and opposite a hill known affectionately as the maiden's breast. Barbara had fallen in love with the place, and so it was for me. Besides, Barbara was pregnant again, a condition made abundantly apparent when she sat bolt upright one night in the small hours and demanded iced champagne. I am sorry to say her curmudgeonly husband denied her the privilege.

The process of learning about gunnery and how to teach it was immensely enjoyable for me, and the summer days passed happily. The evenings were a little turgid by comparison, for I had undertaken a correspondence course to get me through the written captain-to-major promotion exam. This was a less stringent exercise than the staff college entrance exam, which was a necessary prerequisite for selection to Staff College at Camberley. However, it had always been my intention to return to the 'other' staff college at Shrivenham for the Technical Staff Course, and the promotion exam was all that was needed. I saw no need to do more than was necessary, and took the easy route.

In late October, James arrived on the scene, and soon afterwards we left Lulworth for a long family holiday in Beaminster. We discovered that the regiment was on the move again, this time to a place called Homs in Tripolitania, about eighty miles east of Tripoli itself. This time, the family was coming with me.

It was January 1958, and we moved into Number 4 Oleander Avenue, almost 100 yards from the beach. Every room had a friendly gecko on the ceiling to keep down the flies, and we employed a capable Arab cook called Bashia. In truth, Bashia had fallen foul of his previous employers, but he spoke a fair amount of English and I asked him to explain the problem. It seemed to me to be a bit of a storm in a teacup, and I took him on. We were not to be disappointed.

I told him two things. First, my orders to him would come from my wife, but they were *my* orders. Secondly, if he wanted a bit of tea, sugar or whatever, he should ask and he would receive. If that seems a bit medieval, it was how I sought to win his trust at the time. In any case, it got us off to a good start, and he never abused his position. Indeed, he coped manfully with the problems of the kitchen stove.

The stove was an utterly primitive affair that used paraffin to supply three separate wicks grouped under three cooking 'rings'. Success depended vitally on keeping the wicks properly cleaned and trimmed. Failure in this regard would result in what was called a black-out. It happened all the time to everyone. The kitchen would fill with a large nauseous black cloud of minute carbon particles that covered everything, and banished the gecko. The loud shouts of 'black-out!' were familiar in Oleander Avenue.

An even more dangerous hazard was the bathroom geyser. It was the means by which a hot bath was achieved, and required bomb-disposal qualifications of anyone who chose to use it. An upright copper cylinder was mounted at the plug end of the bath, and cold water was fed into it by means of a cock at the rear, out of reach of anyone in the bath. Supposedly hot water would emerge out of a tap which, fortunately, was within reach of the user. The means by which cold water became hot was due to a wood fire which one had to keep going in the interior of the geyser. The speed of gush-out of the hot tap was crucial. Too fast, and the water never got hot. Too slow, and the geyser could explode. Not enough wood on the fire (which could not be attended to while in the bath) and the water stayed cold.

It was undoubtedly a team effort, especially when bathing the young. But on one occasion, after a detailed briefing lasting several days, I eventually persuaded my reluctant batman to prepare a bath for me. I returned to the bathroom in time to see him backing out, while calling ever more urgently: 'Sir! SIR!'. Beyond him, the fire was raging, the hot tap was off, and the geyser was bonging and banging with infinite menace. I flew to the hot tap and somehow escaped the jet of steam which blasted out of it. My batman was nowhere to be seen, and I excused him from bathing duties. We would both stay safer that way.

My responsibilities as Regimental Gunnery Officer were quickly defined for me. The Colonel took me to a site about twenty miles away on the edge of the open desert. It was an area of perhaps three square miles which had real features of hill and valley. Beyond, the desert was endless, flat and lacking in any recognisable landmark. There were two big level terraces reasonably close together which the Colonel identified for me as the two firing points. One would be for AP (armour piercing) practices, and the other for HE (high explosive) practices.

This needs explanation. A round (bullet/shell) of AP was designed to penetrate the armour of a tank. It left the muzzle of a tank gun at about three times the velocity of a rifle bullet, and the concussion of the gun firing was considerable. A round of HE left the gun much more slowly, with a quieter sort of thump, describing a relatively lazy arc on its way up to a 'soft' target of trucks, buildings or perhaps a river bridge. Unlike an AP round, it exploded at the other end. An AP round, however, would cause a bright flash as it went straight through an armoured target. For this reason it was useful to have old tank hulls as 'hard' targets for AP practices, because it was easier to see when the gunner had done a good job. It was also very satisfying if an HE shell exploded precisely on a hard target of this kind, because HE was less accurate than AP and a direct hit scored lots of brownie points for the gunner.

It was important, too, to have separate firing points for AP and HE. The sheer velocity of AP called for a relatively narrow arc of fire and a long danger zone or template. HE could be given a much wider arc of fire and a shorter danger zone - a fatter template.

'You will have just four hard targets to site in any way you want,' said the Colonel. 'Oh, and over there on the skyline you can see a cairn I built which I've called "Tom's Tit". It's around four thousand yards away, and you can use it for a troop shoot. And now it's over to you.'

No gunnery officer could have asked for more. I had this barren piece of terrain to turn into my very own range, and I had carte blanche. What fun it was going to be, I thought, and I was not mistaken.

A most useful piece of information which came my way was that there was a pile of stone blocks out in the desert shaped into one-foot cubes. Precisely what their purpose had been, nobody knew, but they were vital to my purpose. Three of these piled on top of each other would make a perfect marker for, say, the limit of arc beyond which a tank gun on the firing point would not be allowed to traverse. To make them stand out in the glare of the desert sun, it would be necessary to paint the sides of my cubic stones alternately black and white.

The next problem was how to set them out on the range at precisely the right bearing from the firing point, and what should those bearings be. I began by setting up stone markers at each end of the two firing points, and then fixing their positions with great accuracy upon my 200,000:1 map. This was made possible by taking compass bearings of the firing-point markers from up to three other places already marked on the map and which could actually be identified on the ground. There were precious few of these, but the system worked.

Aficionados will realise that doing this sort of thing on a '200 thou' map of doubtful provenance demanded confidence. As time went by, I soon began to have great faith in my prismatic compass, and I reckoned I knew where my firing points were. The next thing was to determine the danger zone. For this I needed to fashion a template for AP ammunition and another for HE ammunition. A template is made to the same scale as the map you are using, usually out of transparent talc, so that the template can be laid over the map without obscuring the detail underneath. The length of the template represents many thousands of yards, and the arc (field of fire) to left and right is a function of ricochet. The same aficionados will be appalled to hear that I hacked my templates out of a piece of mapboard talc with a kitchen knife.

The bearing of the centre line of each template was largely determined by a small dwelling inhabited by an elderly couple, far over to the right of the range area. Knowing this, I began to draw arcs of fire on the map, and the next step was to set out my stone markers on precise bearings from each of the firing points. I needed a 3-ton truck with its driver to carry the stones, a Ferret scout car and its crew armed with a pair of binoculars, and myself with my trusty compass.

With the help of much chat on the radio, I sent the other two vehicles out to a spot about a thousand yards away, so that from where I stood on the firing point, they were well to the left of the spot I was looking for. I ordered the 3-tonner to drive very slowly from left to right, followed by the scout car. The scout car commander stood up in his turret and watched me through his binoculars. The point about all this was that the rear end of a Ferret forms a very sharp profile. When the hard line of the engine compartment coincided with my compass bearing, I waved an arm. The commander shouted 'halt', and with luck we were lined up. We soon got the knack, and when I was satisfied, my distant party of three would pile three stones precisely beneath the rear of the Ferret.

While all this was going on, my Squadron Leader came out from Homs to see what I was up to. He watched our little routine rather superciliously for a while, before he said, 'I take it you're just getting your markers into the rough position you want them?'

'No, this is dead accurate. They are where they should be.'

'I don't believe it! Give me your compass. What's the bearing supposed to be?'

'One hundred and seventeen and a half degrees.'

A minute later, I had proved my point. Empirical methods can be very effective.

During these past weeks, Lieutenant Colonel Peter Vaux had arrived to take over command from Colonel Tom. He had told me to press on with the gunnery range and that, if there was a problem to be solved, I should go back to him. Meanwhile, REME had come to my aid by bringing four hard targets to the range. Positioning these had been another delightful brainteaser, for I wanted to ensure that each firing point could make use of at least three of these targets without coming out of their arcs of fire. With this achieved, the final task was to erect secure range warning flags round the whole perimeter of the danger zone. I reported to Colonel Peter.

It had seemed to me that the enterprise would take three or four days, and would need some sort of safari to achieve it. I had collected large empty oil drums and a concrete mix to pour into them in order to secure the flagpoles. The flagpoles had been fashioned by the LAD, and pulleys had been welded to the masthead. There were halyards and red flags, and an Arab employee with a pot of white paint to write 'danger' in Arabic on each oildrum. My request to the Colonel was for him to nominate an officer to take command of the operation, organize and provision it, and set off into the wild blue yonder to set up the flags.

This was agreed, and a chum went off on a splendid picnic, enjoying every minute of it. As a postscript, I have to say that, not only were the actual red flags removed by locals within forty-eight hours, leaving the poles bare, but anything removable from the hard targets also disappeared in a similar time-frame. The bit that amazed all of us was that this had occurred in an area that appeared almost devoid of human habitation. Which meant there was a quite remarkable bush telegraph in operation.

The day approached when the regiment would begin firing. It was to be a Monday, so on the Sunday it was arranged that Recce Troop, supported by an artillery spotter plane, would sweep the range to ensure that it was clear. Each Ferret carried a Libyan policeman as an extra passenger in case a problem arose. The range was indeed completely empty except for an enormous tented cantonment just inside the far limit of the danger zone. Literally on the borderline, there was a scene of biblical majesty, where an old patriarch had set up camp with his sons, grandsons, camels, sheep, goats, and of course his womenfolk. He saw no reason why he should move.

It took three more days and the help of a very senior Libyan official before the patriarch grudgingly moved his camp the necessary four hundred yards. At last, early on the Thursday morning, I sought permission from the Colonel to 'zero in' our own A Squadron guns. This involves the use of 'service' AP ammunition (that is, operational ammunition instead of the cheaper and slower version used for training), firing at special zeroing targets sited at 1,000 yards. These carry a black grid on a white background, and are used to enable an adjustment of the gunners' sights until the gun puts a shot through the target at precisely the point of aim.

We watched progress through our binoculars for some sixty seconds before one of the tank commanders reported seeing movement downrange through his powerful periscopic sight with x10 magnification.

I grabbed the radio: 'Stop! Stop! Unload, clear guns, green flags up!'

Closer inspection revealed a classic frieze etched against the skyline some 3,000 yards away, right under the guns. It was a young Arab boy with a donkey and three camels. My Squadron Leader and I took a vehicle up to him and escorted a very nervous lad off the area. The moral of the story has to be that the desert is not empty. But from that moment there were no further incidents and we enjoyed an uninterrupted programme of annual firing practice for the whole regiment.

Time was passing very pleasantly. First parade was good and early, probably at six o'clock from memory, and formal activity ended at 1330 hours. Late lunch was followed on most days by a visit to the beach with our sons. The only hazards were the smell from the soap factory if the wind was in the west, and the occasional rhinoceros beetle sliding down one's personal sand dune. Bashia used to visit the market for us and bought meat at a reasonable price. If we had gone instead, the price would have soared. Besides, we were spared the sight of all the flies buzzing around the raw meat.

Best of all, the warm Libyan climate was doing Barbara a world of good, and at last she was recovering her energy and vitality. This was just as well, for we were on the move again. I was to join 12 Technical Staff Course at Shrivenham in June, after a mere six months with the regiment. Bashia's last task was to defrost the refrigerator and in doing so he destroyed it completely. We found him trying to remove the ice with a heavy kitchen knife, whether from impatience or ignorance we never knew. I vigorously denied liability for the replacement of one refrigerator, and fortunately Colonel Peter agreed. He told us to fly home and said that he would deal with the matter. I believe it took him nine months or so to get the wretched thing written off.

CHAPTER VIII

WIDENING HORIZONS

Our points score for married quarters had improved markedly now that we had two children, and had been through quite a bit of separation. But it was still abysmally low, and for two months we had to stage in a minute semi-detached quarter in the section of Watchfield village known to us all as Chinatown. (These days, the semis have all been joined up to make family homes of a sensible size.) Six of our big crates had to be left out in the equally minute garden in all weathers, and many of our books were irreparably damaged.

But in August 1958 we graduated to the relative comfort of a house plumb in the centre of the usual 'married patch', and we launched ourselves into the spirited social life of Shrivenham. As usual, Barbara got herself a horse to ride, which was always a high priority for her. There were several occasions when my friends espied me with my wheelbarrow, walking at a discreet distance behind Barbara as she rode through the village, picking up useful fertiliser for the garden.

I had served with the Commandant before, when he had been Commander of 20th Armoured Brigade in Munster, and I had been Adjutant of the Sixth. Major General 'Shan' Hackett was a man of great accomplishments. One of these was a quite phenomenal memory. As a brigade commander, he would remember not only the name of the corporal standing before him, but also that his wife was on the verge of producing her first baby. I once asked the Brigade Major whether he and others on the staff had a system for briefing the Commander on these things. On the contrary, I was told, it was entirely the personal business of the Brigadier.

In consequence, when General Shan entered the lecture hall for his welcoming address, it was no surprise to me that he should recognize me from behind, and clap me on the shoulder with some suitable remark as he walked past. I had to take quite a bit of banter from the rest of the Course about that.

The aim of the Technical Staff Course was to educate future staff officers in the business of equipment procurement. Those who became students at the Staff College in Camberley barely touched on the topic, grateful that when a problem presented itself in the procurement field, there would be someone with 'technical' know-how whom they could consult. Over the years, this ethos has changed radically, in step with the increasing dominance of technology. Nowadays, everybody on the staff courses spend the best part of a year at Shrivenham.

I have always felt that 'technical' was the wrong word. It has connotations of a bloke who is good at taking the cylinder head off the engine under the bonnet of his old banger, and putting it back again, just for fun. In due course, the phrase 'Weapons Staff' was coined to describe the real function of those who had passed through Shrivenham. It is a staff function which involves, to begin with, the concise and succinct briefing of senior officers on all matters concerned with operational requirements, and the subsequent procurement process which follows, leading to the introduction of new equipment into service. In due course, many of the briefers become decision-makers in their own right, developing wide-ranging links with defence industries in the process.

It is fair to say that Shrivenham taught us a 'language' - the language of the scientist, the engineer, the designer, the production manager and the contracts man. We were required to learn the art of briefing on complex matters *without* confusing the recipient, or losing sight of essentials. We would visit some of the famous firms in the defence industry to see how things were done. And we had a design exercise of our own to undertake, wrestling with all the compromises involved and finally presenting our solution to a senior invited audience.

The full course was one of 2½ years, but graduates like myself joined at the end of the first year for a shorter spell of eighteen months. The first year was spent by non-graduates doing selected groundwork in the fields of physics, chemistry and maths.

As usual, I became involved in an argument over which specialist module I should undertake. A lot of graduates came under pressure to do Electronics and Guided Weapons, and many succumbed. I resisted stoutly, maintaining that to do so would be building castles in the air as far as I was concerned. I was a tank man and wished to remain so. Thankfully, I was allowed to take up the Weapons and Vehicle study. I was never very good at wiggly amps.

Back in Common Close, one of our first tasks was to introduce our alsatian Syn to the boisterous children in the 'patch'. He was marvellously steady, but the young had to know enough not to startle him. He became a familiar presence among the children, to the extent that other parents also had confidence in him and relaxed their vigilance. His natural temperament was superb, and we had trained him using methods written about by the great naturalist Konrad Lorenz in his book *Man Meets Dog*. Basically, when Syn was a puppy and started to do something naughty, like advancing upon an unsuspecting group of chickens to create mayhem, we would grab him by the scruff, lift his forepaws off the ground and shake him, the while telling him 'no'. It was infallible, for one only had to do it once for any given lesson. This is not a method that works with smaller dogs, I hasten to add (a hunt terrier would probably have your wrist off).

I have said that we enjoyed amateur dramatics and we took ourselves once more into that world, discovering all our old friends on the permanent staff with whom we had played before. Another slice of fun came from taking part in motor rallies of the 'noggin and natter' variety. Sometimes it was a matter of getting people lost over a distance of, say, forty miles before finishing at a pub for sustenance. On other occasions it became more difficult, lasting through the night for upwards of 100 miles or so. There were some who got into the big time, and there was a Military Rally based on Shrivenham which the enthusiasts organized with some success.

There was a particularly intrepid team of girls who went rallying, and Barbara was the navigator. They earned many plaudits for surviving a hair-raising night in hurricane force winds. They just avoided crashing into a fallen tree, only to discover that another had come crashing down behind them. They went cross-country to extricate themselves, to enjoy eventually the considerable respect of the male fraternity, who welcomed them back to safety with some relief.

Towards the end of the course, when stress began to build up a bit, two of us added to the turmoil by creating the first Christmas revue, or pantomime, at Shrivenham. A lively sapper called Jimmy Capadose started it, recognizing that Camberley had had this tradition for many years. It was great fun and, I suspect, rather like the curate's egg - good in parts. But then we learnt that General Shan had told our successors on the next course that they would be 'required' to put on a show too. Thus began a tradition which remains today.

As Christmas approached, I saw the Commandant's car draw up outside our house one evening. The driver handed me a note from General Shan to say that a chum called Tim Paton and I had both been selected for automatic entry into the Camberley staff course in a year's time. This was wholly unexpected, and completely changed everything. On first arrival at Shrivenham, I had been expecting to get some sort of staff job. Now, it seemed sensible to return to regimental duty. During our time away, the Sixth had amalgamated with the Third to form the new Third Royal Tank Regiment, with Colonel Peter still in command. They were in Detmold, in the same barracks where I had originally joined the First. I had to be tidied away somehow for about eleven months, and the Third accepted the challenge.

The solution for Barbara and the family was to install them in a flat in a manor house in Shrivenham village until I had explored the quarter situation. With such a short posting, our chances appeared slim. I left the car in England with Barbara and set off for Germany.

It was an extraordinary year. My military involvement included the appointments of Second-in-Command of Headquarter Squadron, Regimental Messing Officer (the one they all dread), the Regimental Liaison Officer at Brigade HQ (during field training), and Officers' Mess Property member. This all seemed rather pedestrian to me, and I recall making a small bleat to Colonel Peter about it. He told me stuff and nonsense, and of course he was right. I learnt all sorts of things while at Detmold that stood me in good stead in times to come.

I made an absolute nuisance of myself about a married quarter, getting right up the nose of the Station Staff Officer whose responsibility it was to allocate these temporary homes. Barbara and I held to the philosophy that one should put up one's wigwam somehow, wherever fortune decreed. I was eventually told that a quarter would be available in June for my last six months. In the meantime, however, kind friends had noted signs of stress, and offered us their quarter while they went on holiday. So we settled into Zeppelinstrasse for the month of March. Fortunately, some more kind friends went on holiday and left us their house in Hoherheckenweg for the month of April (I mention the names, for they have a sort of ring to them, do they not). But for reasons of tax, Barbara had left the car behind in England.

There was still May to sort out, and the only solution was for my Squadron Leader to send us off to the BAOR leave centre at Winterberg, using the Colonel's staff car to get us there. An amazing way to get leave, but there it was. And then in June, we settled into our own place, back in our old friend Zeppelinstrasse, to the relief of everybody who had done so much to help.

Tragically, it was then that Barbara had to endure a miscarriage. The stress of being so unsettled at this time must have been a major contributing factor.

There are always a few unwritten rules about routine inspections. My father used to tell me that, during the Captain's Saturday morning inspection of his ship, there was one item that had no stowage space. This was a very large sack of cotton waste, used to smarten up all the brass. It was carried by an able seaman detailed off for the task, and his mission was never to be heard, let alone seen, by the Captain during his rounds. The Captain, of course, knew all about him, and would sometimes change direction and dive down a companionway in the hope of spotting him.

The army equivalent of such things was enshrined many years ago in a book by Anthony Armstrong called *Warriors Paraded*. I have experienced several of the chapters in that book over the years, and we had one such day when Colonel Peter was due to hand over the regiment to Lieutenant Colonel Allan Taylor. A few days before, the Colonel decreed that he would like an informal walkabout to say goodbye to whomever was in barracks. There were to be no special preparations.

Nevertheless, the cook sergeant-major felt that, once breakfast was over, the cooks should revisit their barrack room and check things out.

Just as well. As I arrived at HQ Squadron block, I could see all manner of detritus flying out of the top windows to descend into the bushes at the rear. Meanwhile I found the squadron leader and sergeant-major helping one of the sergeants to clear up a fire bucket that had just been kicked over near the front entrance.

I was sent off to meet the Colonel outside, and managed to steer him through a side entrance while the sergeant and his fire bucket hid behind a pillar. At this moment the cooks decided to make a quick evacuation down the back stairs and out through the side entrance. The Colonel disappeared from view behind a flurry of white smocks and chefs hats, boots sliding and stamping on the slippery tiles and stairs as a dozen young men strove to avoid barging into the Colonel and come to attention at the same time. There followed much close-quarter arm-waving as they all saluted as best they could in the confined space without poking anyone's eye out. The Colonel sent them off with some good-humoured advice about cooking the next meal.

B Squadron block was next, and since they were all out on training, the Colonel invited me to accompany him. We were met by a smart corporal who declared himself ready for inspection. The Colonel indicated his wish to visit the barrack rooms upstairs, whereupon the corporal saluted and disappeared. We mounted the stairs to the accompaniment of a distant obbligato of pounding boots. We were greeted by the same corporal, now a little out of breath, as he shouted: 'Five Troop, Sir!' and showed us into a barrack room. This continued throughout the inspection, the corporal quite clearly determined to reach our next destination by some circuitous route in order to check that all was well before he greeted us on behalf of another bunch of his absent colleagues.

He flung open a final door: 'The Squadron orderly room, Sir!'

The sole occupant of the orderly room was a small puppy, hock deep in the remains of many important papers, dampened by more than one suspicious puddle. The dismay on the corporal's face is something I will always treasure. And the Colonel thoroughly enjoyed his morning inspection, which continued, I am glad to say, in the same vein.

My time in Brigade Headquarters as Regimental LO during field training was probably the most rewarding. Added to my experience while Adjutant, it taught me a lot about the exercise of command, and the working of radio nets at brigade and divisional level. The Commander was Brigadier Jackie d'Avigdor-Goldsmid, a well-to-do bachelor of impeccable mien and a deep interest in people. This was probably why, on retirement as a major general, he became an MP.

His public relations while manoeuvring a brigade of tanks through the beautiful German countryside was of the highest order. He would always entertain the Polizei and perhaps a group of mayors from local villages to a marvellous lunch in a convenient gasthof. This happened every day, and I did by best to be present. So good were these lunches, I was minded to compose a foolish limerick which the Brigadier rather enjoyed:

> There once was a bold brigadier
> Who said to the general: 'Look here,
> The armour won't punch
> While I'm having my lunch,
> So bloody well keep off the air!'

My penance was to write a limerick for everyone on the brigade staff.

This extraordinary twelvemonth came to an end with our arrival in Camberley at 83 King's Ride, literally the sixth roof my family had enjoyed in the course of one calendar year. It was actually seven if you included a brief Christmas holiday in Beaminster. As an Olympic year, it had been full of unwanted hurdles.

Once again, the atmosphere of Staff College surrounded us, with the considerable widening of horizons which it entails. But Camberley was more vibrant in this regard in comparison with Shrivenham for, in addition to the wide sample of British officers, there were many top-grade students from foreign armies, some of whom would be destined to become involved in revolution back home.

Most of the Brits had been through Sandhurst together, which helped to break the ice. This was just as well, for there was little time for social life outside the syndicate room during the first four months or so. Nor could the bleak common behind the college campus compete with the Vale of White Horse as an environment for student officers with congested brains. It was always much easier to relax at Shrivenham.

In truth, the die was cast by about June, as far as one's immediate career was concerned. By then, the formidable army posting organization run by the Military Secretary (MS) would begin the process of compiling the 'black bag'. This was the list of postings that would scatter our course around the world, most of us into our first staff job, and some back to regimental duty.

Nevertheless, the pace hardly slackened, and it was the writing of formal papers that became my particular Waterloo. I greatly envied the skill of one officer who wrote articles for magazines as a hobby. It might be *Woman's Own*, or perhaps *Blackwood's Magazine*. Whichever, he would sit at his typewriter and immediately bang out an article of the right kind. I suppose he was a journalist struggling to get out. Anyway, the night before a paper was required by the Directing Staff (DS), he would sit down surrounded by beer and cigarettes, produce his paper and hand it in. Invariably it would come back with a congratulatory comment written in the distinctive green ink reserved for the Commandant. My stuff would always come back covered in red ink, after three weeks of agonized effort.

We had to write a paper on morale and, having done so, I took it to this officer for his criticism. His name was Carl Mawby. In his view, I had written all sorts of good things, but whole paragraphs were in the wrong place. I handed in my amended copy, and back it came with the coveted green ink. My long and weary apprenticeship had begun.

We were regularly entertained by visiting speakers. GOC Berlin came to give us a first-hand account of the building of the Berlin Wall. I recall the Headmaster of Bedford School coming to tell us about the value and power of words that had only one syllable. There was a splendid man who dealt with the art of speaking. He was brilliant and hilarious. Without any change in diction or volume, he proceeded at one point to stand on his head, facing away from us, continuing his cheerful homily. He was quite portly, too.

Some of the great captains came to speak, like Mountbatten, Alanbrooke and Montgomery. It was always the custom, of course, to stand up when the visitor was brought in by the Commandant. But it was also allowed that we could continue smoking pipes or cigarettes as we rose to our feet. When Montgomery came, all of us remembered that he had invariably begun to talk with the words: 'There will now be a thirty-second pause while you cough and shuffle your feet, and there will be no smoking.'

After, say, just ten seconds, he would call us to order and begin.

It was a tribute to him that, as he came into the Alanbrooke Hall that day, not one person was smoking. And then, after a short few words he stopped and addressed the Commandant: 'Is smoking allowed in here?'

'Yes, field marshal.'

'There will now be a thirty-second pause while you all light up!'

From that moment he had us in the palm of his hand, and his subsequent oration in the familiar clipped style, full of blazing clarity, was indeed memorable.

Before long, the only thing that concerned us was the end-of-course pantomime, plus the final judgements of MS concerning our postings. Having now acquired the so-called double blue, I was subpoenaed to work for DRAC in Whitehall, in the rank of major, at one of the equipment desks. It was to be a new world.

We lived in seedy elegance in Barkston Gardens, just off Earl's Court Road. It was a big first-floor flat that had come towards the end of a long lease, and so we could afford the rent. I was within twenty-five minutes from the office, which was a great improvement over the long commute up the Bakerloo line to Bushey, where most of the quarters were. If I left the office at seven, say, I was home before somebody who had left at six.

There was an excellent pre-prep school just round the corner called Gibb's which we patronized. We noted that it was very up-market, and *soignée* nannies would turn up in a Rolls Royce or a chauffeur-driven Daimler to collect the little ones. We found ourselves becoming involved with ghastly children's parties that ended with the children coming home clutching a bigger present than the one they had taken with them in the first place. There was always an entertainer.

Eventually we succumbed and ran our own birthday party. I was conscripted as the entertainer. So unruly were our savage little guests that I had to resort to a referee's whistle, appropriately called an Acme Thunderer. When the mums came to collect, I wished them goodbye. All were rendered speechless having actually been spoken to by the entertainer, who looked pretty scruffy into the bargain.

'That's no entertainer,' quoth my beloved. 'That is my husband.'

We recalled with pleasure our birthday party for Jonathan the previous year. We took over the gardens of Minley Manor, which was part of the Staff College in those days. We told the young to come as a red indian or a cowboy, and sent them off into the rhododendrons. It was voted the best party ever by young and old alike, for the adults were able to watch the Farnborough Air Show for free.

In February 1962, our third son Anthony was born, to the sound of hooting tugs, at a maternity ward in Woolwich.

The winter of 1961/62 produced the last of the London pea-soupers. It lasted three days and was very unpleasant. The snow turned black on the windowsills, and people had nasty black moustaches from wearing handkerchief masks. It was the major factor in my deciding to give up smoking, finally and for good. I thought I would fail - again! - due to the hectic nature of my job, but it was alright being busy. It was the marmalade at breakfast, of course, and things of that sort that induced the craving. I was okay after about six months, but it was rather more than a year before I got over the wistful regret of a pleasure lost.

My work in the office was in the field of operational requirements (OR). I spent my time trying to draft the needs of the RAC as sensibly as possible. I dealt with the next tank (which was to be Chieftain) and with anti-tank guided weapons. I would consult with other majors and civil servants who had their own axes to grind, until some sort of draft landed on the desk of my boss. In consultation with many other lieutenant colonels and civil servants, he would have another bash. So it went on, until a select group of generals and civil service mandarins felt moderately comfortable with the result.

Sometimes, though, there would be an opportunity for more positive action. Lieutenant Colonel Peter Tynan, who was an old friend of ours from our time together in Beckett Mess, had taken a prototype guided-weapon system called Malkara to Libya for a field trial. He sent me a telegram demanding a complete back axle assembly for a Mark 9 Landrover within the next five days. It was then Thursday. It was immense fun finding out who had the authority to say what. In the end, DRAC had to sign the executive piece of paper, in the knowledge that a senior financier had agreed, and that an aircraft with the axle on board was waiting at Benson airfield 'with propellers turning'. Having earned a brownie point, it was nice to have Peter Tynan take over as my boss some months later.

In more frustrating vein, there was a day when a piece of paper arrived to tell me that the stock of prismatic compasses was running out and we needed a new one. As we all know, compasses work in degrees, of which there are 360 in a complete circle. Some bright spark in the Gunners wanted to change all that.

I must explain, in defence of the Royal Artillery, that it makes sense for the Gunners to measure any lateral adjustment to their guns using mils instead of degrees (I shall explain). If a shell were to explode downrange a bit off line, a switch would be ordered in terms of so many yards to left or right. A mil is what a switch of one yard would look like when seen from a distance of 1000 yards.

The proposition was that it would make a lot of sense to have the next compass marked in mils instead of degrees. A circular had come round asking us all to agree to this, and it seemed that almost everybody had done so. For the life of me, I could not see why. All other armies, all navies and air forces including our own, the merchant shipping of the world, and all civil airlines would continue to navigate in degrees. I caused a lot of muttering into beer tankards by denying the approval of the Royal Armoured Corps. I forecast that, if this proposal went ahead, a special Defence Council Instruction (DCI) would have to be issued listing the necessary conversion tables for use by the Army when talking to everybody else about compass bearings.

I am sorry to say, that is exactly what happened. It is as good an example as any, on a very small scale, of the heffalump traps that lie in wait when it comes to the business of procurement. It was such a silly thing, but by the time my masters had convinced the generals of the folly of it all, it was too late to stop the process. They could only limit the numbers to be issued. The correct solution would have been to provide two concentric scales in the compass, one marked in degrees and the other in mils, as the Canadians had done. To our eternal shame, the DCI with the conversion tables was published a few months later.

There were frequent opportunities for officials to make trips overseas, usually under a NATO heading. These came round less frequently for majors compared with the more senior ranks, for the obvious reason that it is more cost-effective to fill delegations with decision-makers. But I managed a couple of trips to Paris and one to Copenhagen, before getting down to the serious business of plotting a trip across the Atlantic. It took me eighteen months to convince my boss that there was enough business to justify a trip to the United States and to Canada for the best part of three weeks.

It was exhausting and exciting. I have enjoyed being in America ever since. Lesson One is the culture shock, of course. And Lesson Two is that one always tries to fit too much in. I visited the Embassy, the Pentagon and Fort Belvoir in Washington DC, Fort Knox in Kentucky, Camp Borden in Ontario, Frankford Arsenal near Philadelphia, and Washington DC again for debriefing. The logistics of such a trip are dominated by the time taken to travel distances which are far greater than one expects.

Among a maze of impressions, I recall the remarkable hospitality of a scientist from Frankford Arsenal. Although he knew that he would never see us again, he drove three of us out to his home, an hour away from Philadelphia, in order to entertain us. It was quite difficult to get into his house, for we had to squeeze past a large object under a dustcover in the hallway. This was removed with a flourish to reveal the console of a large electric organ. Indeed, the whole house *was* the organ, and the entertainment which followed was quite bizarre. As our host began to play, the sweep of violins and cellos emerged from the living-room ceiling, the blare of trumpets and trombones filled the kitchen, and the real drums and cymbals of the percussion section crashed away from their site in the stairwell. The teenage daughter of the house, whose room was close to the cymbals, protested loudly to no avail. She was trying to do her homework, poor thing.

For our part, we were becoming peckish, for none of us had eaten since breakfast. Slowly it began to dawn upon us that a meal was not on the agenda. Thankfully our hostess identified the reason behind our somewhat wistful demeanour, and rustled up a bit of welsh rarebit. We gobbled this voraciously. Since my day had begun in the heart of Ontario, I could be forgiven for wondering if it would ever end. And yet the generosity of our host was genuine and wholly unselfish. He drove us back to our hotel in Philadelphia late in the evening, which meant for him a round trip lasting two hours. He probably got three hours sleep that night.

My two years of duty on the staff came to an end early in 1964, and in March I took my family to join the Fifth Royal Tank Regiment in the garrison outside Fallingbostel. This is a town at the western end of the Luneburg Heath, about sixty kilometres north of Hannover. Immediately to the east and south is a large egg-shaped tract of blasted heath known as the Hohne Ranges, used chiefly by armoured regiments in NATO for their annual firing practices. On the eastern edge of these ranges, which are full of wild boar, is Hohne itself, or more correctly Bergen-Hohne, where there is another large garrison. There was a time when the place was called Belsen, for the site of the former concentration camp is only a kilometre or so away. To the north lies the town of Soltau, lending its name to the Soltau Training Area which runs further east towards Luneburg. Every armoured and infantry soldier who has ever served in BAOR knows every square metre of 'Soltau'.

Barbara set about finding a horse to ride, and in due course experienced for the first time what it was like to be in a dingy wood at dawn as a squadron of tanks started up. She was terrified, being quite unable to determine whence the noise came. It is indeed a daunting sound, and Barbara found her way back to the stables at best speed before they ran her down.

For my part, I became squadron leader of HQ Squadron, and found myself on Soltau within forty-eight hours of arrival. It was bitterly cold, with the temperature falling on my first night to about minus 10 degrees Fahrenheit, or 42 degrees of frost in the old parlance. It was a sharp reminder that I was back in operational mode.

Our three boys were now 8½, 6½ and 2 years old. Jonathan, our eldest, had started prep school the previous September, and by Christmas we had discovered that the school we had chosen was falling apart. We had an option to move him immediately to a school called Moor Park near Ludlow, which was literally just being established. It is difficult to get these things right at any time, and we were in the middle of planning our own move to Germany. We got it wrong, and did not move Jonathan to Moor Park until the following September.

Moor Park was, and I think still is, a paragon of what prep schools should be like. It was the inspiration of two men, Hugh Watts and Derek Henderson who, with their wives, a matron called Mrs Holyland and a wonderful chaplain from Downside called Brendan, created a school that one felt was a true extension of one's own home. Their teaching staff were creative and enthusiastic without neglecting the basics, and the end product was a bunch of exuberant young citizens who understood each others' strengths and weaknesses and never bullied.

All that was in the future, and our earlier months in Fallingbostel were coloured by the agonies of having the first-born disappear to boarding school for the first time - and hating it. Yet it was the only feasible option for service families who sought continuity for their children, providing a firm base at the school while 'home' moved at very regular intervals. Service schools existed, but understandably the tuition was at the level of lowest common denominator. The children who went to these schools never stayed for long. They moved about all the time with their parents, losing any sense of continuity in their education, and constantly going over old ground.

Summer leave was a much-needed release from such cares. The Italian lakes beckoned, and our excellent Ford Cortina (I had 'run in' the engine by taking it on a 300-mile rally to the Harz Mountains and back) was well able to absorb the clutter of camping gear. We left Anthony, our smallest hopeful, in the care of good friends in Fallingbostel, and headed south. We landed up at Arona, at the southern end of Lago di Maggiore, in a place which Barbara and I had spotted during a second honeymoon trip some five years previously. The boys decided they liked Italy, and everyone learned how to say '*cinque cento cinquanta cinque*'.

HQ Squadron is half the regiment. A tank squadron is relatively small and well defined, with a collection of tank crews and little else. I had all the rest, a conglomerate of relatively disparate groups doing their own thing, some of whom positively resented any interference from me.

There was Command Troop of course, including the Colonel and the 2IC, the Adjutant and the RSM, the Regimental Signals Officer and his section, and the Assistant Adjutant with the Chief Clerk and the orderly room. They had three tanks, a couple of armoured command vehicles which seated about eight (these were converted personnel carriers), plus a few rover vehicles for the more important personalities and, when we could extricate them from barracks, an office truck for the clerks.

There was Recce Troop with about a dozen Ferret scout cars and a well-developed sense of independence. There was the MT Troop with all the trucks, the Provost Sergeant with his regimental police, the Light Aid Detachment (LAD) of REME, the Pay Office manned by the Paymaster and his RAPC clerks, the Cook Sergeant-Major with his ACC cooks, and the staffs of the Officers' and Sergeants' Messes. Then there was the Technical Quartermaster with his very expensive stores (mobile in trucks) and, doyen of them all, the Quartermaster himself with something like thirty to thirty-five years' service behind him.

All this presented my squadron sergeant-major (SSM) and I with the problem of creating a recognisable identity for the squadron. There was nothing new about this, of course, but the task did seem a little daunting. Sport of all kinds was the best aid to solidarity and, being half the regiment, we often walked away with trophies.

Morning parade was rather different. It was an important aid to discipline, and the only sensible way of getting the day's agenda off the ground. I was amazed to discover the persistence with which such luminaries as the Chief Clerk or the Quartermaster would try to make excuses for their staff being off parade, on the grounds that they should be working at something else. I won 80 per cent of the argument, I think.

A new experience for me was my responsibility as a squadron leader to enforce military law, insofar as my delegated powers would permit. Again, having half the regiment under command, I soon began to marvel at the ingenuity of soldiers as they set about explaining why their late return from leave had been quite beyond their control. One learns, too, of the relatively fine line drawn between the exuberance of an active soldier and the mischief-making of a free spirit in defiance of authority.

Man management plays an enormous part here. A satisfied soldier is seldom a defaulter. We had a petty criminal in the squadron who could get nothing right. He was scruffy, dirty, idle and always in trouble. Then some genius (probably the sergeant-major) put him into the Officers' Mess as a waiter. That trooper became a changed man, wholly transformed into a smart, clean and polite young member of the mess staff whom we could trust with anything. He had found his vocation, and was completely rehabilitated.

* * *

We much enjoyed having an American officer seconded to us, a Major Bob Sunell with his wife Jo-Ann. He got a good basketball team together, and had us all playing mixed volleyball over Christmas. He was the first American to explain to me that a dry martini should be prepared by pouring in the gin and breathing the word 'vermouth' over the top of the glass. What is more, he meant it.

Jo-Ann has never allowed me to forget my first appearance on her doorstep in Queen's Avenue, where we all lived. I was in long white shorts and a blazer, and invited them both to join us for tea and croquet. 'Oh! That was so *English*!' she would declare. She pronounced it 'crow-*kay*'.

Almost in no time, it seemed, our year in Fallingbostel was up, and the regiment began packing up in readiness for our move to Tidworth and Salisbury Plain. The Sunells stayed in Germany and completed their secondment with the Royal Scots Greys.

We moved into a house with three storeys in a fine old Victorian terrace. It was spacious, with high ceilings and well-proportioned rooms, ideal for a family such as ours. We were much relieved to be within three hours or so of Moor Park School, where James was soon to join Jonathan. He was glad to get there in the end, for he hated the school in Tidworth.

Meanwhile, I had taken over B Squadron, at last getting back to real tanking after a gap of no less than eight years since our time in Homs. I soon learnt that I was to take the squadron away to an independent station at Castlemartin Ranges in Pembrokeshire for three months. Once again I was to be of service to the Territorial Army, this time lending my own tanks to the visiting armoured regiments for their annual range practices. We were all delighted with this, but the downside was our enforced separation from our families for quite a lot of the time. Part of the solution for Barbara was to get a horse.

When the TA had finished with us, the other two squadrons came out in turn and used my tanks to do their annual firing. Eventually we got our property back and conducted our own firing before finally packing up, leaving the ranges clear for the German panzers. They had started to use Castlemartin in 1961, and continued to do so for thirty-five years, bringing much business into the area.

Castlemartin was a lovely place to be, close to nature and with magnificent sea views. There were clouds of guillemots (known to the Welsh as ellegugs), razorbills and puffins to observe in our free time, as they chattered and argued on the sheer rock pillars sticking out of the sea. I managed to get the family out for a bit of very windy camping, and lost a brownie point or two by returning at night to the comfort of the mess. There was some obscure reason for that, but it cannot have been a good one.

As the autumn approached, we began preparations for a major divisional exercise in Libya called Exercise Dazzle. My part in this was to serve as an umpire. However, during the preliminary period of desert training, there would be an opportunity for me to do a navigational trip across the 'bulge' of Cyrenaica from a point west of Tobruk to a point south of Benghazi. I was to be joined by John Ellis, the Adjutant, and a small party using two rover vehicles. This gave Lieutenant Colonel Peter Day the idea that I might make an amateur film for recruiting purposes during our time in Libya.

I am not a photographer of note, let alone a film director with an advertising bent. I warned the Colonel of the risk he was running, but he stuck to his guns. I took the best advice I could, and bought a very expensive movie camera and the right sort of films. I made an outline plan and got on with things.

It soon became apparent that there were only two occasions in the day when filming was possible - early dawn or late dusk. There was no contrast at all under the merciless desert sun, and this limited my options. But I got some quite good silhouettes of tank crews keeping watch from the turret and so forth, and cooking the breakfast meal. Eventually we set off on our desert trip, which we enjoyed immensely. Unfortunately, when we got back to base, I discovered that the film I had used during our desert voyage was for indoor use only. The Colonel was remarkably understanding. He just said it was a funny thing to do for an officer who was supposed to be 'technically aware.'

Deep in the desert during the big exercise, as night was falling, John Ellis came through on the radio from RHQ some twenty or thirty miles away: 'Reference your posting to Shrivenham in two months' time - cancel.

You are to report to FVRDE in one month's time. Quarter available - wife informed - over.'

The Fighting Vehicles Research and Development Establishment was the home of tank design, situated near the village of Chobham between Sunningdale and Chertsey. I had been looking forward to seeing Shrivenham again, and did not want to go to Chobham, as we used to call it. I was very angry and set off back to RHQ to see the Colonel. It was the only cloudy night we had experienced, and of course I got lost. Nor could the Colonel help me, so I had several stiff gins and got back to my umpiring.

When I got back to England, I rang the Brigadier who was to be my new boss and asked him what was going on. He said I was going to California.

CHAPTER IX

CALIFORNIA

For Barbara, the news also came as a bolt from the blue, but in a quite different way. She was out for a walk in some woodland when she came across June Dey, the Colonel's wife.

'Oh my dear!' said June, 'How *are* you going to cope with Simon being away in America for six months?'

'WHAT?!'

'Oh . . . gosh . . . didn't you know?'

Barbara was shattered. This was very bad news as far as she was concerned, with yet another move and yet more separation. This was going to be a real test of marriage. Somehow we found a way of transporting Barbara's horse to Heathlands, our new home near Chobham. There was nowhere to put it, so it had to go in the garage, which was conveniently spacious. Happily, Heathlands was a rather fine old house set in its own garden of about two acres. We filled the top floor and another family had the ground floor. There were to be a couple of months or so before I set off for sunny climes, and Barbara did her best to concentrate on the positive things.

I, of course, was frankly delighted at the prospect of going to California although, like Barbara, very sorry not to be returning to Shrivenham as a member of staff. But I still had to find out what this California thing was all about.

At about this time, the Army were considering how best to replace the ageing reconnaissance fleet of Saladin armoured cars. The designers at Chobham had come up with an excellent blueprint for a whole family of vehicles, starting with a recce vehicle mounting a 76mm medium-velocity gun. A similar variant would mount a 30mm cannon. Other turretless variants would provide an ambulance, a command vehicle, a recovery vehicle and a small infantry section vehicle. The generic name given to this particular requirement was Combat Vehicle Reconnaissance, or CVR. A notable innovation for this type of vehicle was to make it front-engined. Apart from the turreted versions, all the other variants needed a door at the rear, and the front engine meant almost 100 per cent commonality in the hull for the whole fleet.

Working to the same timescale, the American Army had drawn up a specification for an armoured scout vehicle (ASV), at about three-quarters the weight of a CVR. The Canadians were very interested in ASV, and the Australians were very interested in CVR. The generals scented an opportunity for a collaborative enterprise between the four countries, which were already bound by treaty into a thing called ABCA (America, Britain, Canada, Australia).

It was decided that a six-month Feasibility Study should be awarded to the Ordnance Division of a well-known American company called FMC, and that Canada would take the lead. There was to be a military Quadripartite Working Party stationed with FMC as a means of controlling progress. I was to be the British representative. The aim of the study was to examine the possibilities for commonality between an ASV and a CVR. For example, there seemed to be a prima facie case for a similar chassis, with perhaps an extra road wheel inside each track of the bigger CVR. FMC were supposed to find out for us.

The FMC plant in question was located in San Jose, some fifty miles south of San Francisco. I could hear the siren songs already, and I got out some books about California. To my dismay, they told me about black widow spiders and cone-nosed bugs. So I bought some maps instead, which have always fascinated me, and pored over the outlines of San Francisco Bay.

Meanwhile, planning and briefings filled my time, both at Chobham and at the headquarters of the Director General Fighting Vehicles. This was in Southwark, in a building called St Christopher House, half of which belonged to the Ministry of Defence. It was from here that I received my formal orders. One of my main concerns was to try and get the allowances right. This was a completely new enterprise as far as the men in green eyeshades were concerned, and I had some difficulty in getting them to think positively about my potential needs. We never did get it right, to the extent that I nearly petitioned the Army Board when it was all over. I eventually took the view that, while I was out of pocket to the tune of about £200, I had been greatly privileged in getting to California at all, let alone to the vicinity of San Francisco. At least, that was my argument for chickening out and not bothering the great men with my whinges. Frustratingly, I learned eventually that my allowances *could* have been got right if the people concerned had thought a little more about it.

Sometime in late January 1966, I was summoned to Ottawa for a week's conference. I had a very pleasant weekend with an old chum from the Sixth and his wife, Tim and Dinny Green, who were enjoying a posting to the High Commission. It was mightily cold and I envied the Canadians their sensible clothing. My British Warm, long johns and a scarf were barely enough for the task, but some vigorous tobogganing with the Green family restored my circulation.

The Canadians had called our international working party together for the first time, and had organized a programme of briefings for our future task. So began some lifelong friendships. Colonel Bud Betts of the Canadian REME was to be our Chairman. Captain Hal Wyant, our Secretary, had spent quite some time in North Vietnam, working for the UN during the war years. Then there was Major Joe Ameel of the US Cavalry from Fort Knox, and Lieutenant Colonel Ian Gilmore of the Australian Sappers, from the Australian Embassy in Washington. I was introduced as a Lieutenant Colonel, but my rank was purely honorary. I think my masters thought it might give me more clout. This was not the case as far as the Working Party were concerned, but it came in useful in other unexpected ways, as I shall relate.

We were to report to FMC in San Jose early in February, and we returned to base to start packing.

Barbara and I decided to buy two identical tape-recording machines to communicate with each other. It seemed a good idea to offer a weekly forty-minute dialogue, listening to the voice of one's beloved, instead of the usual letters. This worked very well, although we found that forty minutes was a long time to fill with news.

In those days, travel was by commercial airline to New York, and then a short hop to Washington, where the compulsory briefing took place at the Embassy in Massachusetts Avenue. My guide and mentor there was Lieutenant Colonel Carl Barras, RTR and I was to become most grateful for his help on more than one occasion. He showed me a large map of the States with lots of coloured pins in it, giving the whereabouts of the many British Liaison Officers scattered about the country. With some ceremony, Carl Barras stuck in a pin for me, a good thousand miles to the west of anybody else. Such independence was wonderful to have - nobody was going to descend on me unawares - but I learned in due course that I was to miss the advantage of trotting down a corridor, so to speak, in search of help and advice.

I was put on a plane at Dulles International airport and began the exciting trip across the States under clear blue skies. Most unusually, I was able to see the ground almost all the way across, looking down from nearly 40,000 feet and spotting the major features using the large map supplied by the airline. We curved north to begin with towards the great lakes, crossing Lake Erie south of Detroit and Lake Michigan north of Chicago. Continuing westward over Iowa, one could see the easily visible Missouri River, where it becomes very wide north of Sioux City. The prairies seemed featureless, but then came the Rocky Mountains, followed by some 700 miles of desert and mountain, including the Salt Lake in Utah. At last we crossed the great Sierra Nevada and started to sink earthwards over the last 200 miles, down towards the magical setting of San Francisco. I vowed that Barbara would have to see it all herself one day. I was like a schoolboy let out for the holidays, and when, in later years, I was to introduce others to this experience for the first time, they all reacted with the same slack-jawed excitement.

The final hop to San Jose was by helicopter along the bay, over multi-coloured saltings and extensive fruit orchards to the airport next to the FMC plant. There I was met, I forget by whom, and taken to our little motel on the Alameda, in the neighbouring town of Santa Clara.

The St Nicholas Motel was quite small and enclosed in the form of a square, with just two storeys. There was a tiny swimming pool at ground level, and a sun terrace on the top level. Our rooms opened out onto this, and made for extra harmony among our small group. Joe Ameel brought his vivacious wife Betty with him, for they had no family to worry about, and she became Mum. The first thing she did was to buy me a teapot.

Ian Gilmore was allowed out of his Embassy for a week every month, and in his absence I was to watch over the interests of the Australian Army on Ian's behalf. Keeping an eye on us all from her redoubt on the ground floor was the chatelaine of St Nicholas Motel, the formidable Mrs Anderson. It was as good a set-up as we could have expected.

Only one thing was wrong. I had no car, whereas of course everyone else did. We were about two miles from FMC, there were no buses or taxis to be had where we were, and there was no question of my walking along the freeway. I tried to explain these things to the Embassy staff in Washington, as they expostulated over my ridiculous request for a car. Nobody seemed to see the incongruity of the poor Brit being lifted everywhere by other members of the group, including trips to the shopping malls and, worst of all, the twelve miles to the naval air station at Moffett Field where I was obliged to go to send 'UK eyes only' messages. Carl Barras did his best on my behalf, and tried to get London to help. London, of course, said it was the business of Washington. Washington went on saying that, if the Military Attaché (a major general) could not have a dedicated car, then on what grounds could this upstart in San Jose be treated differently?

I won in the end. Months later, an old chum called Leslie Douglass who had been my squadron leader in Detmold, and who worked in St Christopher House in Southwark, told me the following: 'It was quite difficult, Simon, when walking across Blackfriars Bridge on a bitterly cold and wet February morning, to sympathize with a message from sunny California blabbing about an "intolerable situation over car"!'

The funny thing was, I was directed to Los Angeles to pick up my hired car, some 350 miles south. So in the end I enjoyed a flight down the coast, a visit to the wonderful dolphin displays at Marineland, and then a happy two-day trip back up the coast by way of Big Sur, Carmel and Monterey.

We soon settled into a very pleasant routine, professionally rewarding, and with plenty to see and do at weekends. We enjoyed frequent visits to the drawing office, where we pored over engineering drawings and debated the merits of different designs with the chief project engineer. The executive director in charge of the project, Chuck Johnson, remarked that we had been sent to answer their questions and, golly Moses, that was what we were doing with the minimum waste of time.

A certain high flyer in FMC called John MacRostie began to take a close interest in us too, and he organized informal Friday gatherings over lunch in a bar somewhere, to exchange notes on progress. Known as 'Big John' in the company, he was the divisional director for research and business development. Here began another lifelong friendship, cemented at parties in the neighbouring small town of Los Gatos, where John and Barbara MacRostie lived on the edge of the Santa Cruz Mountains. John had designed their house himself and, being smack over the San Andreas fault, he had had earthquakes in mind. But the lasting impression I have from many subsequent visits is of the spectacular view from their living room across the San Jose valley to the Diablo Range ten miles to the east.

In those days, San Jose housed some 100,000 souls, and there were extensive orchards everywhere. In due season, every filing cabinet in every office sported a basket of apricots, picked that morning off the trees in private orchards. So I learned what an apricot should taste like. Nowadays, the orchards have gone, and the population must be approaching one million.

I kept meeting British employees of the company. There was a draughtsman who had been working in the San Jose plant for just three years when I met him. He had begun with FMC in Chicago or Minneapolis, but had been attracted by the thought of moving to California. After just three years, he was living in a house to his own design on a mountainside somewhere. I could hear the siren songs getting louder and louder.

To my intense relief, the principal designer in Chobham was told to come and join our group for the month of April. Les Monger was something of a legend, and generals used to hang on his words, even while he was telling them they were talking poppycock. No one else had the courage to do this, which was why Les was always paraded up front at big meetings. The process at FMC had advanced to the stage where the engineers were wrestling with turret design for our vehicle. FMC were brilliant on matters to do with mobility, but knew virtually nothing about turretry in those days. I was also getting out of my depth, and the appearance of Les Monger in San Jose was mightily welcomed by all parties.

In the nicest possible way, Les tore up the FMC turret designs and began to sketch out something that looked remarkably like our own CVR turret. My personal contribution had been to insist that the vehicle designed by FMC should have an engine installed at the rear, so that my masters in UK could compare the result with our own front-engined design for CVR. Besides, the US needed a rear-engined vehicle too, for their ASV, and we were in the business of trying to achieve commonality. Slowly, a rather dinky looking vehicle began to emerge which greatly impressed my chum Joe Ameel. He was having a bad time trying to help FMC with the very difficult ASV specification. The shape emerging from the FMC drawing boards looked extremely odd, and I began calling his vehicle 'the hunchback of San Jose'.

For some time I had been plotting the arrival of my entire family in San Jose for the Easter holidays. Basically, this meant the month of April, and I duly booked the best suite in the motel. The whole thing was possible because of the privilege of obtaining 'indulgence flights' with the RAF. To my surprise, I discovered that the RAF came regularly to San Francisco on their way to Christmas Island in the Pacific. To quote a famous remark by a distinguished officer in the regiment, I 'moved with the speed of a striking snake' and the scene was set.

Two days before the day of the flight, the RAF telephoned Barbara to ensure that all was in order. It was not. Jonathan had developed an appalling temperature, and Anthony's smallpox vaccination was somehow not in order. The trip was cancelled, and there was a lot of misery about.

Les Monger and I went off on a couple of trips together. The first was based on an official visit to a Lockheed plant east of Los Angeles, in order to learn more about a somewhat eccentric rough-terrain vehicle which really did have triangular wheels. The hidden agenda to this trip was a visit to Disneyland at Anaheim, which opened my eyes to the excellence of that particular enterprise. The proof is in the pudding, in that one emerges from a day-long indulgence without feeling exhausted. Compare this with a single hour tramping round any city.

Our second trip came with the Easter break, now sadly without my family. We travelled by car the 150 miles or so eastward to Yosemite Canyon in the high sierras. The trip took us through the Diablo Range and across the wide San Joaquin valley (pronounced San Wahkeen). Yosemite is a wonderful place (it has four syllables with the emphasis on the second). The snows were beginning to melt high above, and the waterfalls were at their most majestic. Blue jays were everywhere, and the sheer cliffs sweeping vertically upwards for 3,000 feet swamped the imagination. And we saw our first racoon.

Back in Santa Clara, the Ameels were challenged by my assertion that I had not yet seen a knickerbocker glory. I have no idea where I got this from, but I knew it to be the rolls-royce product of any soda fountain. The Ameels were mystified, which pleased me greatly, and I began to show off by describing one of these things from the active pool of my imagination. The next Saturday I was marched off to the nearest soda fountain where the product of my dreams was awaiting me. It was about a foot high and took me a full half-hour to consume.

The real honeypot was San Francisco, made infinitely more accessible once one had summoned the courage to drive a car downtown. It was like driving up and down ladders, with fabulous views opening up on all sides if one knew where to go. Once on foot, a favourite thing was to take the external elevator up the side of the Fairmont Hotel at the top of Nob Hill. As the contraption rumbles upwards, the city slowly opens up below, revealing new vistas eastward past the huge Bay Bridge to distant Berkeley, and north to Alcatraz. The restaurant at the top was called the Crown Room, justifying the name by having plastic replicas of our own Crown Jewels on display. Seen from the windows of this rather exotic spot, the Golden Gate by sunset remains one of the most romantic sights in my experience. The dry martinis were also extremely expensive.

There was much more, of course. We took cable cars to Fisherman's Wharf, and visited Gump's, the 'Harrods' of San Francisco, off Union Square. A trip to Vista Point at the northern end of the Golden Gate, followed by lunch in Sausalito at the Alta Mira, is a recommendation I have made to many people, all of whom have reported upon the experience with acclamation.

While San Francisco is exciting, Carmel is beautiful, like a Spanish St Ives nestling among the cypress trees. It lies just south of the Monterey peninsula, with Monterey itself to the north. The road round the seashore from Monterey is called 17 Mile Drive, past golf courses where the first requirement for membership is to be a millionaire. The most famous of these is Pebble Beach, just to the north of Carmel. Very unlike the Royal and Ancient at St Andrews, it is permissible as a complete stranger to walk into the Pebble Beach clubhouse, which is called the Del Monte Hotel, as though one was a member. There, one can order a drink, eat a meal looking out over the myriad purples, greens, blues and violets of the Pacific, and finally stroll down to the edge of the eighteenth green to watch the members play. I asked John MacRostie how this could be, and after some thought, he replied: 'Well, California's a big place, and there aren't too many people in Carmel, day by day.'

Long ago, a Spanish Jesuit called Father Junipero Serra established seventeen mission churches along the Californian coast. The best-preserved of these in its original, unrestored state is at Carmel, and I treasured the occasions when I could get to Mass there. Otherwise, the Ameels and I used to attend another of the mission churches, now much restored, which served the University of Santa Clara, quite close to our motel. Father Serra now has a freeway named after him, which seems a touch incongruous.

There came a time when the Director General Fighting Vehicles and the Director of the Fighting Vehicles Research and Development Establishment at Chobham were due to visit us as part of their official liaison tour round the States. The DG was Major General Ray Leakey of the regiment, a gallant officer with a distinguished war record. Mark you, Barbara had it in for him because he had been responsible for sending me to California in the first place, but that is another story. Part of my duty was to fix them up with hotel bookings in San Francisco, and General Ray invited me to join them for dinner on the Sunday evening of their arrival. Some few glasses of whisky later, I was patted on the shoulder and told to get back to San Jose in readiness for their arrival the following day.

It was then midnight, and by some miracle I found my way onto the freeway going south. It was solid in all four lanes. Moreover, it was trying to rain for only the second occasion I can remember. Suddenly I became aware that the vista of car rear lights in front of me had become brake lights. I braked suddenly, but the drizzle had turned the road to grease, and since the freeway was curving left at that point, I carried on in a straight line, coming inexorably closer to the line of cars on my right.

While I managed to stop before hitting the car in front, I had already bounced neatly off the sides of two cars in the neighbouring lane. Both were driven by Chinamen, who leapt out to tell me that I had hit their cars, with which I could only agree.

By Californian law, the Chinamen remained where they were, blocking their lane. This seemed silly to me, so I manoeuvred over to the hard shoulder in what I thought was a public-spirited gesture. In no time the Highway Patrol were upon us, and I played my cards as only a British army officer would - wholly reasonable and willing to help. I stank of whisky.

As soon as they heard my accent, the message went forth, and I was squeezed between two large gentlemen in the back of my car, and two other patrolmen came to sit in front. I continued to use the English language to the best of my ability, and they seemed to enjoy the entertainment. I worried about the whisky, though. Finally the guy in charge said, 'Waal, I guess there ain't no injury here, no fisticuffs, and it'll be down to insurance, huh?'

They very kindly showed me where I could get my fender straightened out, and bade me farewell. Joe Ameel could hardly credit my story when I told my chums all about it. Not only did I not get a ticket, but they allowed me to drive back. This was unheard of, and of course Joe never let me live it down. As for the General, he thought it was the best story he had heard in a long time. Lucky me. I have no idea how the Chinamen fared.

From time to time, Joe got into real difficulties with his masters in Fort Knox, who cared nothing for the enterprise in San Jose and wanted him back at base. When this happened, the rule of thumb was that Bud Betts, our leader, would telephone Ottawa, and I would ring Carl Barras in Washington. Carl would then contact the key Lieutenant Colonel in the Pentagon, and so would Ottawa. The result was a curmudgeonly climb-down by Fort Knox.

There came a day, though, when Joe received a direct order by telegram to report to Fort Knox immediately. This was a different matter altogether. Fort Knox was trying to call our bluff. We spent an entire morning discussing the wording of a truthful reply from Joe that would serve to buy time while we mustered our defences. This was a more difficult one for the Pentagon to solve and, as I recall, Joe actually returned to Fort Knox temporarily. Meanwhile, his boss came to see us in FMC, and we did our best to persuade him that we needed another couple of months to finish the job, and Joe would be free. It was on occasions like this that it helped to be an honorary lieutenant colonel.

Meanwhile, we began planning for the final four-nation conference in August, and it became apparent that I should return to UK for a fortnight's leave, in the course of which I would be grilled by my masters. This was a marvellous thing for Barbara and I, and it was great to get my proper centre of gravity back. The siren songs became fainter.

For the final three weeks, Ian Gilmore brought his delightful family to our motel for a holiday. His wife Alison and a young cousin of his, together with Betty Ameel, created a strong feminine element in our group at a time when we were beginning to plan farewell parties, and the Gilmore children brought a splendid family atmosphere into our tiny motel.

Ian and I planned a joint party, using up vast quantities of duty-free Beefeater gin and Johnny Walker Black Label, together with appropriate supplies of English beer and Australian lager. The other thing was to be sausages, but these did not exist in our neighbourhood. However, a willing butcher listened to our specification and supplied some for test. We purchased twenty-one dozen and choked everyone into incoherence with the fumes from the barbecue that cooked them. We had some very good parties, and there began to be some sadness.

We spent a glorious six months proving that the enterprise given to us was impossible. It was early days in the collaborative business and lessons began to be learnt. The real gain from our efforts was the personal network which we had forged, helping us to understand each other's systems and methods, of so much value for the future. We buried the project with honour, and returned to our homes.

CHAPTER X

WE ALL NEED LUCK

There were some good things and some bad things about the next nine months or so at Chobham. It was great to be happily restored as a family, with a comfortable quarter, and my hours in the office were not long. The Officers' Mess was rather grand, sited in the extensive central reservation of the test track area. If that sounds insupportable, it was not so. The outlook from the terrace of Barrowhills, as it is called, was full of woodland, with a nearby open-air swimming pool and a golf course. As for Barbara, she was able to ride out on Chobham Common and, together again, we began to recharge batteries. There is no doubt, too, that my time at the Establishment was of real value to me in later years, because of the acquaintances I made among the researchers, designers and developers on the staff. Chief among these, of course, was Les Monger. But it was difficult to appreciate this at the time.

In professional terms, I felt that I had become lost to the Army, for the Military Secretary had never intended me to be sent to Chobham on a formal posting in the first instance. I had been earmarked for Shrivenham. My arrival at Chobham was simply a means of getting me to California on a special project. The job I had been given on my return was not rewarding. Even my confidential report went badly for me. The brigadier who wrote it had taken over, during my absence, from the brigadier who had first been told to send me to California. This guy knew nothing of what I had done in the States, and gave me an unjust grading. I was told that my senior reporting officers would restore the balance, but some damage had been done.

There was also the wretched battle over allowances, and the cumulative effect of all these silly things tended to take the gilt off the gingerbread. Fortunately, my sense of humour never deserts me for long, and we got on with things. But I needed luck.

* * *

The first bit of luck came at a cocktail party. Where this was and who gave it has been lost to the fickle jade of memory, but it was a crucial milestone for me. It was there that I met a chum called Roy Dixon who was by then commanding the Fifth. In the course of conversation, he was airing his concerns at not having a regimental second-in-command and the difficulty he was having in getting someone posted in.

'Colonel,' I said, 'I would absolutely love to be 2IC of the Fifth if you will have me.'

'But Simon, aren't you being saved for one of these new project manager jobs that are being set up to handle equipment procurement?'

'No. Those jobs are to be filled by full colonels. There is no impediment I know of. Please may I come to the Fifth?'

'Watch this space!'

My posting order came through in a remarkably short space of time. I was intensely relieved, and off we went again to make a home in Tidworth for the second time. It was great to be back with the gang.

The second piece of luck came the following October, when it transpired that Roy Dixon would be required immediately for his next staff posting. Moreover, our next commanding officer, the charismatic Dickie Lawson, could not appear among us for some four months or so. The unusual consequence of this was that I became Acting Commanding Officer for that period, as a major. The element of luck, perceived only in hindsight, was that the Royal Tank Regiment as a whole were about to celebrate the fiftieth anniversary of the Battle of Cambrai. As things turned out, this was to give me a high profile within the regimental hierarchy.

It soon became apparent that we should have to move into the CO's tied quarter, if only to make it possible for us to receive and entertain the aforesaid hierarchy. So we left Plantation Road and settled into the cavernous interior of Candahar House. There was a housekeeper (who kept our boys very much in line), a gardener and a wonderful steward called Corporal Mitchell. Of him more anon.

As to the business of command, I found myself surrounded by a cheerful and supportive soviet of majors who very soon adapted to my way of doing things. The mantle of commanding officer was not nearly so daunting as I had thought it might be. As the Cambrai celebrations approached, the experience of past years served me well, and vigorous preparations were set in hand. Chief among these was the need to prepare a welcome for all three Colonels Commandant. There was General Sir Alan Jolly, at that time serving on the Army Board as Quartermaster-General, Major General Jock Holden, and Major General Bill Liardet. All of them were to stay, with their wives, at Candahar House.

Corporal Mitchell took me in hand. We began in the dining room, where Mitchell explained that a bell was located under the table at one end. Clearly, he expected me to sit at that end. I disabused him of this, and told him that the mistress of the house would sit there. He was somewhat alarmed by this, having been used to a bachelor household under Roy Dixon. He rallied manfully, however, and instructed Barbara in the system of signals. One ring to recharge glasses, two rings to clear away plates, and three rings for emergencies.

Next, we allocated rooms, including one for Bill and Betty Fairbairn, whom we had invited to help restore the average age of the impending gathering and, basically, to hold our hands. Everything began on an extremely cheerful and relaxed note, and we went in to dinner in high good humour. One of my character defects is that I get talking too much and, without realizing it, I sat down firmly at the bell end. I gabbled happily away during and after the soup course, until I became aware of Barbara gesticulating wildly at me to hurry up and press the bell. Mortified, I reached hurriedly for the bell and gave it the treatment. Within seconds, Corporal Mitchell rushed into the dining room. He was armed with a stirrup pump and a fire bucket.

The generals and their wives thought this was the best demonstration they had seen for a long time, and were profuse in their congratulations for a drill well performed. Corporal Mitchell is one of the nicest chaps I have ever met, but I fear that he may never have forgiven me.

The generals began to say how awful it was that we had been lumbered with them, and swore they would make an early departure the next day. We told them no, and that there would be a leisurely breakfast beginning at 9 o'clock in the morning. Being a stickler for timing, I turned up for breakfast with Barbara and the Fairbairns at precisely 9 o'clock. There was a contented munching sound from the hierarchy, who were being quietly attended to by Corporal Mitchell.

They had almost finished breakfast. Moreover, important staff cars were crackling over the gravel outside, and in no time they had all shot off in a cloud of dust. Well . . .

But we had given them a good time, and it was probably the first time in my young life that I came to realize how much senior officers enjoyed the normalities of service life at regimental level. What really upsets them is pomposity, and we gave them none of that.

Next on the agenda was the move of the regiment to Germany, this time to Wolfenbuttel, which is just south of Braunschweig (Brunswick), some way east of Hannover and only half an hour north of the beckoning Harz mountains. Once again, I found the mechanics of moving the regiment familiar to me from past experience and, early in the new year of 1968, we arrived without mishap in a quite different world.

I should say first that we were no longer an armoured regiment with tanks. It had been the turn of the Fifth to become an armoured reconnaissance regiment while in England, and we continued in this role in Germany. We were equipped with Saladin armoured cars, and we were to be the eyes and ears of the Corps Commander in our sector, in the event that the Soviet Union decided to invade.

There was an added interest, in that we were close to Helmstedt, where the autobahn lifeline to West Berlin crossed the Iron Curtain. In a different sort of emergency, we had a role to play alongside French and American troops to reopen the autobahn if access to Berlin became denied to us. We used to practise this about twice a year, and we would assemble a tri-national convoy in our barracks before taking part in some sort of exercise. Every vehicle mounted the three national flags on the mudguards, and I rather enjoyed going round telling various miscreants that they had our Union Jack upside down. It is the sort of thing I can spot at a range of a thousand miles, and my countrymen are just as bad at getting it right.

Not being superstitious, we enjoyed our year in number 13 Im Hasenwinkel, or 'hare's corner'. A sizeable stretch of woodland came up to the fence at the bottom of our garden, and the attractive little town of Wolfenbuttel was just down the way. Our relationship with the local populace was subtly different compared with previous experience. It was all a matter of the solidarity which came from living together so close to the Inner German Border. There was also that indefinable sense of freedom which comes from being well separated from everybody else – the nearest army barracks was forty miles away. We set about doing our own thing.

In terms of recreation, this meant skiing in the Harz mountains. We had never done this in our family, and I marshalled Barbara and the boys to join me in this new experience. There was plenty of advice to be had from the younger officers, and we soon kitted ourselves out before high-tailing to the nursery slopes. Unfortunately, one of our first lessons seemed *not* to be on a nursery slope, but on a near-vertical stretch of sheet ice with a precipice at the bottom. We insisted that this should not be repeated, and the young officers lost interest as we retired to safer havens near the delightful town of Braunlage.

But it was a strange experience for Barbara, who had spent a lifetime falling off horses in a way that would have drawn applause from the Parachute Regiment. She never found the solution to falling off a pair of skis, which clearly makes use of different principles, and for her the après-ski was the highlight of the day. I have to say that I also enjoyed the cosy combination of schnapps and Pilsner beer (carefully monitored, of course) in the warmth of a local gasthof, to the accompaniment of a bowl of thick oxtail soup and rough granary bread.

Our boys were steadily growing up. Both Jonathan and James were still at Moor Park, but Jonathan was due for Downside in the autumn, and rather dreading the change. Young Anthony, now six, was old enough to join us on our next major expedition south of the Alps. We promised him the warm waters of Lago di Maggiore, hot sun and blue skies, quite spectacular mountains, and plenty of that wonderful Italian ice cream.

For the first time in our experience, this did not quite work out. The thunderstorms that often rattle around the high peaks in midsummer decided to come south and give us a drenching – more than once. And I wasted a complete morning trying to contact the regiment by phone after hearing of the Russian intrusion into Czechoslovakia. When I finally got through and requested orders, I was told to lie back and enjoy the holiday. Everyone is quite relaxed up here, they said, stay cool.

At the end of our tented holiday, the weather turned violently uncooperative, and we had to pack up in some disarray, with sodden canvas and wet clothing. We were in need of succour, and we rang up old cavalry friends who had since left the Army to settle themselves close to Turin, pursuing a new career. Marvellous warm baths restored morale, and we were introduced to pizzas as they should be made, in a bread oven.

The impact of Dickie Lawson upon the regiment was immediate. He had won considerable acclaim as the officer who had rescued a party of nuns in the Congo some years previously during the uprisings there. Armed only with a walking stick (we called it an ash plant) and a good straight left, he biffed a belligerent rebel soldier on the nose, to the huge amusement of the other natives, and spirited the nuns away by air before the mood changed. This had earned him a DSO - but that was only a part of his reputation.

In my opinion, he achieved great things by doing everything in precisely the opposite way to everybody else, and getting away with it. He was a very fine leader, and he wasted no time in bouncing the Fifth into life in a way not given to many men. He made the corporals of the regiment organize an officers' training day, and he sent Barbara and I off to Copenhagen to establish how the soldiers might enjoy a holiday there as cheaply as possible. An unusual approach, to say the least.

By adjusting the training schedule to run over a number of weekends, the Colonel was able to decree a five-day break in lieu, giving everybody a chance to get away and do things properly, like a trip to West Berlin up the autobahn. We did this with our boys, who were wholly enthused by the rigmarole we had to go through at the Helmstedt checkpoint, and again at Babelsberg on the outskirts of the city. After a thoroughly boring 100-mile trip at a rather slow average speed, along an autobahn full of potholes and with nothing whatever to see except the River Elbe, the transformation at the other end was spectacular.

Barbara and I had been to West Berlin in our first year of marriage, before the Berlin Wall had gone up, and again while we were in Fallingbostel in 1964, but the city never failed to enthral. The first impression was of a blaze of light and a non-existent speed limit, certainly as far as the Germans were concerned. Like moths to a candle, we would wander into the brilliant Kurfurstendam and on, past the elegant ruin of the memorial church, looking for those wonderful little shops where one could pick up some excellent china from East Germany. A trip through Checkpoint Charlie into East Berlin was de rigeur, to absorb the uncompromising bleakness.

But the boys remember the quite excellent zoo, the food and the sights, and the minor traffic accident in Kantstrasse. We were looking for a pizza house, and Jamie suddenly gave a great shout of 'pizza!' I turned my head to ask where, and - bang! Would I never learn?

It was a short and amusing year but, like many such postings where people are thrown together miles from anywhere, a year was probably enough. Besides, at last, we were off to good old Shrivenham again where, on promotion to Lieutenant Colonel, I would join the Directing Staff as DS Armour. Before I left Wolfenbuttel, the Colonel gave me an outrageously good report which I did not deserve. I smelled a rat, but luck seemed to be favouring us once more.

The year 1969 was one in which we lived in five different houses. For the first six weeks we were still in Wolfenbuttel. We had asked for an unfurnished quarter when we got to Shrivenham, for we had by now inherited quite a lot of stuff. So we occupied a furnished quarter for two months until an unfurnished one came free. This was our third roof, and undoubtedly the finest quarter we had ever had.

However, we were gluttons for punishment, for we frightened ourselves into taking out a mortgage on an old Victorian vicarage just under twenty miles away. This was to be home for our teenage boys, and the place where we would begin to put down roots. House number four.

And then the unbelievable happened. I was selected to command the First, which had been my starting point with the regiment. This was incredible news and wholly unexpected. Then I began to wonder whether, perhaps, my previous confidential report had been made sufficiently generous to restore the balance against that earlier unjust report from Chobham, and so make it possible for 'the system' to accept a recommendation for command. I will never know, of course; but the bottom line was that the regimental hierarchy wanted me to don the mantle that every officer covets.

And so for the last three days of 1969 we lived in our fifth house, which was in Osnabruck, Germany. I took over command of the First on 1 January 1970.

CHAPTER XI

COMMAND

Taking advantage of tax laws which allowed one to import cars without duty if kept for at least a year overseas, we invested in a Triumph and a Mini. By the time we came to leave the Old Vicarage, we had lived there for a mere six weeks. My mother had come to help, and had spent all her time making curtains. Somehow we celebrated Christmas, and then immediately drove Mother back to her fastness in Cornwall, before setting out on 28 December for Harwich. We left the house empty, hoping we could rent it out to somebody. The cars groaned under the load of two adults, three boys and an alsatian called Lara, plus an incredible amount of kit. There was black ice everywhere, and we only just made the ferry.

By this time we had come to know that the civilized way of getting to Germany was by the overnight ferry from Harwich to Bremerhaven. It cost more, of course, and the young men still relied on the much shorter and sleepless route through Ostend or Zeebrugge, followed by a long drive. The older ones amongst us, though, had come to appreciate a good night's sleep after an excellent smorgasbord supper, and a sumptuous breakfast in the morning.

The First were stationed in a northern suburb of Osnabrück, within easy reach of open countryside, We were pleased with our quarter, which followed the solid two-storey German pattern with a spacious basement and an equally roomy attic. Unique to our house was the existence of an extra double bedroom and a bathroom occupying part of the attic level. We understood it had been put there by some previous cavalry commanding officer, and very useful it turned out to be.

Osnabrück was a big, prosperous city with many imposing towers, churches and civic buildings. It housed the largest garrison in the British Army, including HQ 12 Mechanised Brigade, ourselves, two battalions of infantry, two regiments of sappers, an RAMC field ambulance and a REME workshop. There were a number of other smaller units, plus a large NAAFI presence and a SSAFA sister. Our relationship with the German authorities was well structured, and the First were 'twinned' with a small town called Georgs-Marien-Hütte. We eventually learnt how to pronounce it.

Osnabrück was situated far enough south and west to escape the flat monotony of the north German plain. Instead, we could enjoy the attractive rolling country that lay between two long, narrow ranges stretching east and south towards Minden, Bielefeld, Detmold, Hameln and Paderborn. Our barracks were up on a hill, too, and it was a good place to be.

No two commanding officers operate the same way. I know I did some things differently from my predecessor, and the same will have been true for my successor. A regiment is always rife with speculation before a change of command, and it takes a week or two for everyone to settle down to the peculiarities of the newcomer - the quicker the better, of course.

I recognized in myself that I had no driving ambition for higher command. I was quite set on pursuing the specialty of equipment procurement, and I found it easy to accept the important guiding principle of putting the regiment first before any kind of personal ambition. I wanted the regiment to be efficient and happy, and sought to achieve that aim without giving myself an unduly high profile. The real stars among us cannot fail to have a high profile, of course, but such men know how to handle their talents and become role models for the rest of us. Sadly, though, there are some for whom ambition takes over, thrusting individuals who seek to ride roughshod, often at the expense of others. Happily, I have completely forgotten the names of those whom I may have thought were cast in this mould. In this context, I always remember the wise words of a distinguished member of staff at Camberley: 'If you're good at something, don't go round telling everybody about it - just let it come as a wonderful surprise!'

I was very glad to have had my run-in at the Fifth two years previously. One always hears the comment that commanding a regiment is the closest one will ever get to being a god in this life. What is meant by that is that one's slightest wish, once expressed, becomes law. Heady stuff, but dangerous to the unwary. The justification for this kind of sentiment probably comes from the clear knowledge that the buck stops with a commanding officer. Everyone who is either senior to him or junior to him knows this. And the strange thing is that the effect upon me was to make me as relaxed as I have ever been. It is the loyalty that gives one the courage.

More than this, one is uniquely at the centre of a very big family. Old comrades are spread all over the place, with a powerful focus in the recruiting area. For me, this was mostly in Liverpool and its environs, with a strong sprinkling from Leeds. The latter had come about because, a few months earlier, the Fifth had been disbanded. Their strength had come from Yorkshire, and many of the Fifth had come on to the First because of our northern connections. The mixture of the white rose and the red rose was potent indeed.

So, as a born southerner, I relished the bubbly cheekiness of the Scouse, and the contrasting slow deliberation of the Yorkshireman's wit - and thought carefully about what I wanted to do.

It had been my experience to be thrown into the deep end from time to time, and I decided to do much the same with my squadron leaders. Within the broad dictates of my own policy directives, I wanted them to draw up their own programmes for training. My intention was to observe, criticize and correct. As with anything else, there are risks to this approach, and I recall that my perceptive brigade commander spotted what I was doing and gave me most valuable advice. The main thing was to ensure that mistakes occurred in relative privacy on suitable terrain. When the CO says go back and do it again, things can get quite messy when a squadron of fifteen or so tanks are involved.

Another thing I did was to turn my attention to the business of providing a guard of honour every time a senior officer came to visit, which was pretty often. I saw little relevance in doing it the infantry way, with much stamping of feet and cleaning of kit. We operated from vehicles, and I invited the Adjutant and the RSM to devise a way of offering the courtesies using Ferret scout cars from Recce Troop. This they did admirably, aided by the presence on site of the RTR Cambrai Band, a real bonus in all sorts of ways. The rest of the regiment greeted these plans with acclamation, being thus excused this particular chore. Whereas Recce Troop themselves regarded the whole thing as a proper acknowledgement of their undoubted professionalism and skill.

It was done with four Ferrets, and part of the sequence involved the guard commander being driven forward to within a few feet of the visiting VIP, where he saluted and requested permission to dismount for inspection. The eight men involved were dressed very smartly in immaculate black denims, with neck scarves in the regimental colour of red. My heart nearly failed me only once, when Field Marshal Sir Richard Hull came to see us in his capacity as Colonel Commandant, Royal Armoured Corps. Whether it was done for a bet I know not, but on this occasion the driver stopped only about twelve inches from the great man, who never flinched. It was I who flinched. Fortunately the driver did not do it a second time when the moment came to seek permission to drive off parade. It was a little ceremony much appreciated by our visitors, especially those who were tank or recce men themselves.

The Services have always put spiritual needs ahead of mental and physical ones. The problem lies in how best to handle it. For my part, I let it be known that there would be no marching to church on Sundays, as it were, and the matter would be left to individual preference. What I did do, though, was to cause a gathering in the gymnasium from time to time on a Friday, as a replacement for squadron morning parades. A minister would come along to give us a hymn, a reading, a thought for the day and a prayer, lasting at the most ten minutes. My excuse for bringing the regiment together in this way was to identify the occasion as part of routine training. As it turned out, the Anglican chaplain was by far the best at this sort of thing.

I used the same explanation when the regiment went onto the Soltau Training Area for, say, a month of tactical activity at squadron level. I insisted on a drumhead service in the field, with the band brought up from Osnabrück, and a flagpole erected in the centre. Three ministers took part, and we finished at sunset with the evening hymn, and the Union Flag coming down to the sound of the Last Post. I believe most profoundly that an occasion like that leaves its mark on all comers.

And then there were the ladies. I freely confess that I had tired long since of stag dinner nights in the Mess. The human race has two sexes, and the best of our fun is enjoyed in each others' presence. I decreed that

Ladies' Nights would be the norm. Moreover, I reminded everyone of the time-honoured custom that precedence over all others shall be given to any bride of less than one year. This was a splendid wheeze when senior guests came to enjoy our hospitality. There was much merit in having some young beauty yapping happily away at the guest of honour, a man many years her senior, for the duration of a sumptuous dinner. I recommend the practice without reservation.

Shortly after our arrival, one of the squadron leaders who had been with me in the Fifth was due to move on, and he had a caravan for sale. We leapt at the opportunity, and we bought it from John Ellis at a price falling not too far short of the amount he had paid for it initially. Likewise, when the time came for us to leave the regiment, our selling price dropped only a small amount below the purchase price, so good was the market value of caravans in BAOR.

This transformed our approach to holidays. We felt we had tried the tenting scenario for quite long enough, and the time had come to be more comfortable. We had our adventures, though, caused mainly by the number of gearbox failures we had to endure. To be blunt, our Triumph motor car must have been manufactured at 1645 hours on a Friday afternoon, and we got through four gearboxes before we were through.

Never mind, we had a secure home wherever we stopped, voluntarily or involuntarily, and we invaded Italy with soaring spirits. Our target was a camping site on the Tuscany coast opposite the island of Elba. We saw Florence and Pisa on the way, and Barbara nearly fell off the leaning tower from vertigo. In the camp itself, we were given a marvellous site close to the endless beaches, with umbrella pines shielding us from the sun and wild rosemary growing all around. It was from there that we took a very successful day trip by coach to Rome, giving me the opportunity to return to that pillar under the Portico of St Peter's where, thirty-six years previously, my father had made me stand following my stubborn refusal to enter the basilica. I behaved better in 1970 and joined my family in the majestic interior, marvelling over the sights that had met my father's eye. And so it was possible to compare Michelangelo's rather stiff *pieta* in St Peter's, sculpted when he was in his twenties, with his unfinished *pieta* in the duomo in Florence, created in his seventies, so very different and wholly remarkable in its composition.

These Italian holidays were a great boost for our boys. We had long since become conscious of the turbulence we inflicted upon them with, on average, a move every year. On top of this, six times a year, they were either going to school or coming back for holidays, involving a journey that quite often had to be accomplished on their own. Some of these trips could become a real adventure. Notable was the beginning of one Christmas holidays when, among a large party of military parents, we had gathered at Hannover airport to receive our young. We were told that fog had aborted take-off for the lollipop flight from Gatwick, so the children were to be taken by bus to Harwich, ferried across to the Hook of Holland, and brought by train to Hannover twenty-four hours later. They arrived grey-faced but triumphant, full of stories of how a bunch of Scottish soldiers had taken them under their wing and seen them safely through the various checkpoints.

Back in Osnabrück some years later, I asked Jonathan how he felt about all this. He was sixteen at the time. He remarked that he had found boys at school who seemed never to have moved more than a hundred miles from their home all their lives, whereas he had enjoyed the opportunity to see Libya, numerous places in Germany including Berlin, a bit of Italy, and quite a bit of England, with places in between.

He went on to say, 'Besides, home is always where you and Mummy are.'

We were mighty pleased to hear that observation, because it was always what we had tried to achieve.

The pace in BAOR was always hectic, some said too much so. It was a matter of fitting together routine training and maintenance, whether inside or outside barracks, annual firing, major exercises, an annual administrative inspection, and all the sport one could manage. The latter depended partly on tradition and very much upon vigorous leadership by enthusiasts. The trouble was, one usually attempted too much, and if a regiment began to get somewhere in a particular competition, whether it be water polo, athletics, boxing, football or whatever, time had to be found for team members to go away and compete for glory. On top of all this were the extras involving special duties, VIP visits, leave, practice emergency turnouts and, last but not least, regimental occasions.

I can recall only one occasion when I firmly opted out of anything. I was required to host a divisional cross-country championship, but in doing so I declined to enter my own regimental team. There was no way we could have coped. But it took some courage, for the divisional commander had been a fine cross-country runner in his day. I lost a brownie point, I think.

There is the dilemma of how to approach things like skiing - does one support the gladiators or the amateurs? Some regiments have had traditions going back years, and regularly devote considerable resource to a small team of downhillers who go away for long periods and come back with trophies. In my case I backed the amateurs, and sent off about 200 soldiers in small parties over a period of about two months to enjoy an ecstatic fortnight of ski training on short skis. This was a most successful BAOR enterprise known as Snow Queen, but we had to find and administer our own regimental chalet near the selected ski resort. This had been done by my predecessors, and I happily supported this tradition.

As usual, out of all this turmoil of stimulating activity, some professional and some extra-mural, there emerges a rich seam of anecdote, endless in its variety, and fundamental to morale.

I have said that generals thoroughly enjoy visiting units, because they recharge batteries immediately in the company of British servicemen in their own environment. The first time General Sir Michael Carver came to visit was an excellent case in point. He and I had never met previously, and when we did so on the tarmac of Gutersloh airfield, he seemed grey with fatigue. This was not helped by a very dodgy trip by helicopter over the Teuterberger range to Osnabrück in swirling mist and bad visibility.

But we got him into the peace and quiet of our house for an unhurried buffet lunch, and we began to discuss his programme. In due course he looked up with a keen eye, spotting the arrival of his Ferret escort outside the house. And then his face lit up with a delighted smile - 'This always happens to me,' he said.

Rather to my dismay, not far behind the escort came a German refuse lorry with three drunken German dustbin men yelling their heads off in amiable but tuneless entertainment. They passed noisily by, full of mock salutes, as we came out of the house and settled into our staff cars. And then, unavoidably, our rather grand convoy had to mount the pavement and bump past the noisy pantomime as it continued its merry way. General Carver began his visit in high good humour and, I'm glad to say, came to see us again some months later.

There was another occasion when the Divisional Commander came to see for himself the progress we were making with an experimental way of accounting for food in the cookhouse. This was not a brainchild of ours, but a rather odd scheme that had emerged out of the Ministry of Defence, and we were the guinea pigs at regimental level.

The General, dressed informally, accompanied the RSM and myself to the cookhouse. He chose a table at random, flung down his brass hat, and sat down. He fixed a beady eye on a rather morose scouse trooper - who took no notice - and the following conversation ensued:

'I take it you come quite often to the cookhouse?'

'No, sir.'

'Just from time to time?'

'No.'

'Were you here yesterday?'

'No.'

'Breakfast this morning?'

'No, sir.'

'Why are you here now?'

'Well, I 'eard yer was coming, so I thought it might be better!'

While the General learnt little from that gentleman, he went away chortling over the incident.

A rather different sort of visit occurred when I chose to invite the Lord Mayor of Liverpool to Osnabrück, accompanied by the Lady Mayoress (who, in Liverpool, has a status of her own above and beyond that of escort to her husband), plus the Chief Executive of the Council and Mrs Holmes. This was all to do with recruiting PR and, to be honest, the chap I truly wished to impress was Stanley Holmes, the power behind the throne. Some years later he was knighted for his services, and I came to understand how richly he deserved that honour.

The party stayed in our house for three nights, and during that time only one message came for him. This was to the effect that the gravediggers of Liverpool had gone on strike, and how should the consequences of that be handled?

'This is the sort of thing that happens to me,' he said ruefully. 'For those families who will not accept a cremation, I must somehow explain that the only alternatives are either to arrange a funeral far away, or to use a system of deep-freeze storage - and where will I find a facility like that of sufficient size? Many hundreds of people die in Liverpool each week. May I use your phone?'

The highlight of this visit was a mess dinner, and for this the Lord Mayor's Sergeant-at-Arms came on duty, being the guardian of the civic regalia. The Lord Mayor had a special chain for grand occasions, but that of the Lady Mayoress was a marvellous jewelled affair of very great value. The lady in question was quite a personality, a blunt but vivacious lass who knew how to drive an HGV and had got on extremely well with our tank drivers. Moreover, she had learnt the mayoral rules of conduct and, as far as she was concerned, they were paramount.

During the preliminaries in the ante-room, the regalia remained concealed in the hands of their burly escort, a point that had escaped me. When all was ready, the familiar sound of the 'roast beef of old England' came from the band and, in time-honoured fashion, I held out my arm to the Brigadier's wife, tipped the wink to the Lord Mayor, and set off in relaxed mode across the hall into the dining room. Nothing else happened, and we looked about us in embarrassed solitude.

I was told later that there had been a significant ceremony during which the Sergeant-at-Arms had satisfied himself that the guests of honour had been properly caparisoned, the while everybody else crushed into a perplexed traffic jam all around them. At last the procession got going and made a most stately entrance into the dining room, where my companion and I had been reduced to giggles. It was the only time that evening when mayoral protocol took precedence over the military equivalent, but not without something of a fight.

The Brigadier was given a hard time by the Lady Mayoress, who wanted him to tell the band they were too noisy. She found it hard to accept that, while I was junior to him, the Brigadier nevertheless regarded the evening as mine and not his, and refused to pass on any advice about the band. But they were having much more difficulty preparing her for the arcane procedure whereby, near the end of proceedings, my wife would catch the eye of the ladies and march them off to the loo, leaving us to our port. This was an essential manoeuvre because our 'Ladies' only had one throne, and use of the 'Gents' was imperative.

The Lady Mayoress would have none of this. 'I go where he goes,' she said, indicating the Lord Mayor. It took a serious talking-to from Mrs Stanley Holmes to bring her under command. When the moment came, the ladies swept majestically away with a mutinous Lady Mayoress, and we sat down again with some relief. Sadly, when I turned round, there was no sign of the Lord Mayor. I am told that he drifted off into the loo, to be surrounded by scandalized women who drove him out. He came back to us eventually, suitably mortified.

The visit was, in fact, an outstanding success and paved the way for an enterprise on the Mersey the following year.

I had conceived the idea of floating a Chieftain tank across the Mersey from Birkenhead to the Liver Building, to be greeted at the famous pierhead by the Lord Mayor (a different guy by this time). We could not land there, and so the tank would have to float back again and come through the Mersey Tunnel on a tank transporter for display in a central square of the city. As a PR exercise it seemed to have merit and was certainly original. Rather to my surprise, absolutely nobody put up any objection.

The Sappers were enthusiastic, for it provided the local Territorial Army sapper unit with an excellent training exercise. They would build me a standard Heavy Ferry, designed for use on river crossings. Stanley Holmes threw his authority behind it, to the extent that some parking meters were removed to create access for the tank onto the centre of the chosen square. The Port Authority was run by a retired naval commander, so there was no trouble there. The Chief of Police asked his experts about letting a tank transporter loose in the tunnel, and gave me clearance. A friendly cavalry commanding officer in Catterick allowed me to borrow one of his tanks and then (he chewed his lip a bit over this) paint our own insignia all over it.

All I had to do was to instruct my young recruiting liaison officer to pick a day when the tide was full but slack at noon, and issue the invitations, including one to Miss Liverpool.

Martin Sinnatt, who was commanding the Fourth at the time, told me he had heard I was doing something crazy on the Mersey, and sent

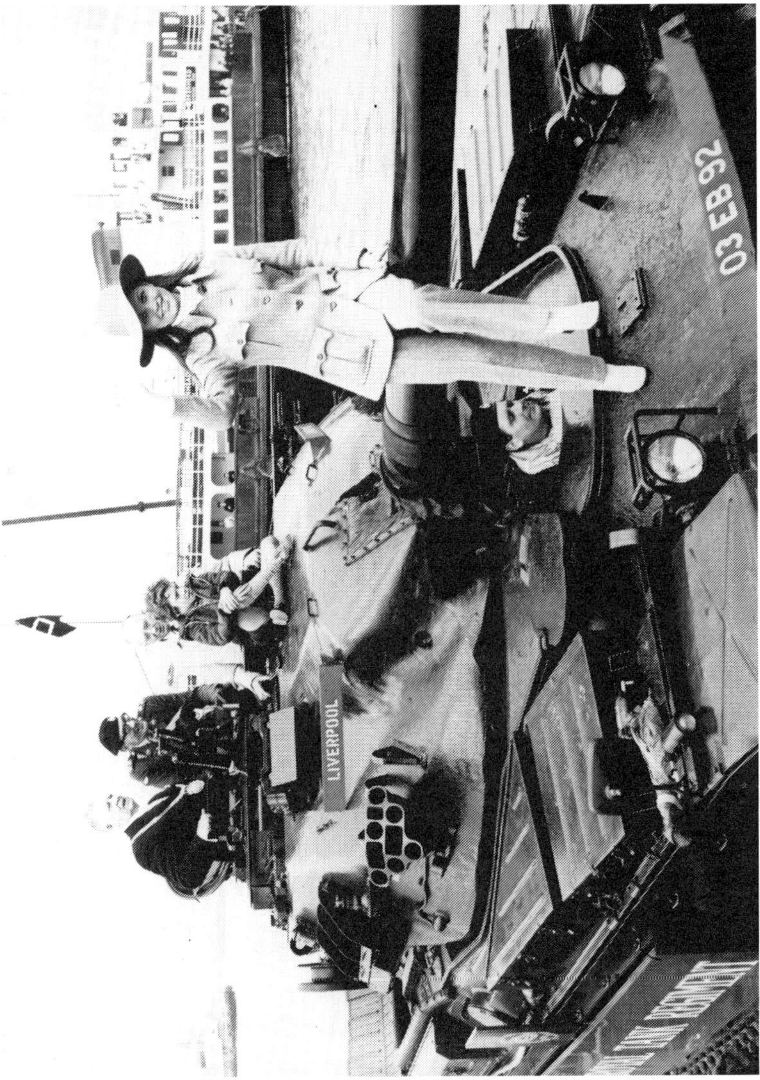

The Author with the Mayor of Liverpool, the Chief Executive, young Bobby and Miss Liverpool after crossing the Mersey by Heavy Ferry on a Chieftain tank. The driver is Sergeant Harry Dennison.

me a letter he had received which he thought I might be able to do something about. It was a childish scrawl from a Liverpool boy called Bobby, and it said: 'Dear Army, I am very keen on tanks and would like to get a ride on one.'

I briefed my liaison officer accordingly. And then the great day came. At the last minute the Chief of Police felt a sense of foreboding and called for another sight of the mathematics concerning the tank transporter in the tunnel. It was so marginal that he reversed his decision, and asked that we cross over by the Runcorn Bridge a long way upstream. This meant a recce in the small hours by my willing liaison officer, who was looking forward to meeting Miss Liverpool again. She was extremely easy on the eye and, rather to our disappointment, foreswore hot pants and appeared in a very elegant trouser suit. She was a sensible girl who knew her Mersey for, although the weather was fine and sunny, a brisk little breeze produced relatively chilly conditions and there was quite a lot of splash.

The crossing went excellently, and we held up all the civilian ferries, whose passengers had a grandstand view. I was not allowed to forget the humiliation which then befell me. My regulation leather shoes were incapable of finding a grip on the steeply sloping metal ramp. My arrival before the Lord Mayor and his citizens lost all dignity as, bent double, I clung desperately on to Miss Liverpool. She glided smoothly onto the pier, dragging with her a most un-officer-like creature with arms, legs and ash plant flailing wildly.

Sure enough, young Bobby was there with his parents, and in due course we all clambered back onto the heavy ferry for a photograph. This time, Miss Liverpool and I made a better fist of our return to terra firma, while Bobby and his family went happily back across the Mersey for the ride of their lives. I have no idea whether the experience caused Bobby to enlist a few years later - one never does know these things, but good luck to him for writing that letter.

Meanwhile, we repaired to the magnificent Town Hall for a major reception and a lavish mayoral luncheon. I yielded Miss Liverpool to the liaison officer, and we all went home content.

The previous Christmas, as usual, we had exchanged cards with American friends from my time in San Jose. The card from Joe and Betty Ameel came from Germany, and I wrote at once to alert them to the fact that we were only a couple of hundred miles apart. The initial outcome was a reunion in the depths of winter, and the chance for me to introduce my entire family to them. And then, a few months later, Joe sent me an invitation to his Command Parade. He was about to take command of the Third Squadron (equivalent to a British regiment) of the Seventh Cavalry.

The US Army have their own traditions for this kind of thing which, as one might expect, are quite different to ours. When a new commanding officer takes over, as Joe was about to do, a formal parade takes place to enable the outgoing CO to introduce the new guy to the unit. The American hierarchy are invited, and the saluting dais groans under the weight of senior officers of the US Army. Joe insisted that Barbara and I should attend. Two seats were reserved for us on the aforesaid dais, and there was no way were we going to miss the event.

It meant getting up very early in the morning and we set off at 4 a.m. with two staff car drivers to share the load. We got there in time and, as Barbara and I took our places I am told there was comment among the ranks: 'Who's the guy in the brown suit?'

It was a very pleasant occasion, and I chuckled a bit to see one or two soldiers wearing sunglasses during the march past. But my driver swore that, from his own vantage point, he had seen one guy with a cigar in his mouth!

Be that as it may, it was clear that minor levities were permitted on these special occasions, in much the same way as our own regimental celebrations on Cambrai Day permit a degree of relaxation in some of the normal disciplines. I have told of another of my American friends, Bob Sunell, who was seconded to the Fifth in Fallingbostel. He was with us for Cambrai Day when, amongst other things, the officers and sergeants always wait upon the corporals and troopers during a lavish lunch party. Poor Bob was struck by a passing bread roll and called for the miscreant to be put under arrest. We had to explain that, just for that day, the rules were different. And of course he understood, but rather wished someone had told him beforehand.

We do not have anything like Joe Ameel's Command Parade. What usually happens is that the CO-designate visits the regiment informally for a couple of days, perhaps a month or two before he is due to take over. He gets shown around, meets all the gang, most of whom he will know, and makes his number with the Brigade Commander. An important item is a full briefing on the forthcoming year's training programme, the timings of which, in BAOR anyway, he could do little to influence. When I came to handover, I had already left the First in the competent hands of the Second-in-Command, and was back in London giving my successor a lift up the Finchley Road after lunch. He got out at a red traffic light, and I told him he could have the regiment.

'Thanks Simon,' he said, and disappeared.

Every commanding officer will suffer at some time from the misplaced enthusiasm of his flock. It happened to me during one of our periods of annual firing on the NATO ranges between Fallingbostel and Bergen-Hohne. The programme usually extended over a fortnight, during which the regiment lived under canvas at a suitable spot just off the concrete ring road that provided access to the individual firing points.

A feature of these ranges, which form a part of the Luneburg Heath, is the wide prevalence of peat, sometimes many metres deep. Range fires were often started by the pyrotechnic content of our ammunition, and special range roads were built to provide access over the peat bogs for the fire-fighting units. These were controlled by the German officer commanding the ranges, a certain Oberst von Notts, whose concern for the wild boar on the ranges transcended most other matters. While many of us sympathized with him over the wild boar, he was somewhat eccentric and an unashamed autocrat who wielded immense power.

During the intervening weekend of our firing programme, a keen REME craftsman was repairing one of our wheeled recovery vehicles known as a Scammell, named after the firm who manufactured them. The job done, he took it off for a road test along one of the special fire-fighting access roads. He probably thought the scenery would be more interesting than if he had motored off along the concrete ring road, which would have been the sensible thing to do. The road went on a long way so he decided to come back, and manoeuvred off the road in order to turn round. The Scammell sank deep into the peat and bogged.

He summoned another Scammell plus a few colleagues to help him effect recovery, but the second Scammell bogged too. The next on the scene was a tracked recovery vehicle, a variant of the family of armoured personnel carriers used by the infantry. One Scammell was recovered before the tracked vehicle itself became bogged. A second tracked recovery vehicle was called to the scene - and hunkered down to join the others.

Nothing daunted, it was decided to report matters to a REME sergeant with a request for an Armoured Recovery Vehicle (ARV) to come and help. An ARV in those days was a specialized tank of about 55 tonnes. When this had been bogged, a neighbouring cavalry regiment was asked, at sergeant level, if they would lend their own ARV to help solve what had become a major incident. After the friendly ARV had inevitably followed the rest into the mire, the men concerned thought for the first time that perhaps they had better inform an officer. By this time the road over the peat bogs had been completely destroyed.

The following morning I visited Colonel von Notts with my tail between my legs. He was quite affable, making remarks about misplaced enthusiasm, and showed me his photographic record of the many disasters that had occurred before mine. We parted in relatively good humour. But an hour or two later, the Brigadier came up to me on the firing point and asked me what the hell had been going on. I gave him a blow-by-blow account and told him not to worry, for everything was now under control.

'I'm not so sure about that,' he replied. 'Von Notts has only one route for reporting things like this, and that is on a direct line to the NATO Army Group Commander. So the Commander-in-Chief knows, the Corps Commander knows, the Divisional Commander knows and I know.'

'Oh,' I said.

'Yes,' said the Brigadier.

I am sorry to say, the recovery had become an engineer task, and the sappers were given an unplanned training exercise lasting a fortnight to repair the road over the peat.

Cambrai Day, 20 November, tends to follow a time-honoured pattern, with minor variations between our constituent regiments. Early in the morning the troop officers and sergeants would wake the slumbering junior ranks in their barrack rooms with 'gunfire' - tea suitably laced with the hard stuff. There would be a drumhead service on the parade ground, or perhaps a fiendish officers versus sergeants hockey match. In any case, the officers and sergeants would gather in one or other of the Messes for drinks before taking on the cookhouse, and dispensing a major feast to the troops. The afternoon might be taken up with the hotly contested final of a sporting competition, in our case football, accompanied by much tomfoolery and dressing up in pantomime gear on the touchline.

Close to Cambrai Day, both the Officers' and Sergeants' Messes would seek to run a dance. These were big affairs, with invitations sent far and wide. But on Cambrai Day itself, our custom in the First was to allow each squadron to run social evenings in their own squadron clubs. This meant that the RSM and I would begin a long evening in the Sergeants' Mess before sallying forth to visit each club in turn. These were good parties, and one of the few occasions when I could get to drink a pint with the troopers.

An exchange I recall with the greatest pleasure occurred while I was doing just that. One of the troopers near me came up and said, in his rich scouse accent: 'Excuse me, sir. Do yer moind if I asks yer a question, personal like?'

'No,' I said. 'Go ahead.'

'Well, is it true, sir - yer was once a trooper?'

'Yes, quite right. I was, for about six months.'

He looked me up and down and said, 'Yers done alright fer yerself, ent yer!'

People tend not to recall the dates of other people's wedding anniversaries. And so it was with Her Majesty, our Colonel-in-Chief. No one knew that her anniversary coincided with Cambrai Day - except me, for I had enlisted on her wedding day. So one of the things I did near the end of my time in command was to alert the RTR to the fact that Cambrai 1972 would coincide with a royal silver wedding. Much discussion followed on the subject of an anniversary present, but one suggestion of mine was accepted. This was that our gift should be a means of helping the Queen to meet more of the young soldiers, rather than, as so often happened, a senior group from the regimental hierarchy.

When a regiment enjoys the privilege of having the monarch as Colonel-in-Chief, the opportunities for bringing the monarch through the barrack gates, as it were, are quite limited in comparison with all other royal persons. The occasion is often quite a grand affair including a major parade, with little lasting opportunity for more casual encounters between troopers and their Colonel-in-Chief.

The anniversary present took the form of a sculpture in silver of a tank crew inside a tank, but with the armoured shell removed. There was a young officer, a lance corporal and two troopers. I was told later that four men representing that crew, together with the Colonel, the RSM and our three Colonels Commandant, visited the Queen in Buckingham Palace to hand over the anniversary present and, by arrangement, to receive it back from Her Majesty for safe-keeping.

I met the lance corporal and the two troopers a month or so after that event in a pub near Bovington. Their faces were a study as they described how they had spent upwards of half an hour with the Queen, chatting away with a pint of beer in their hands. Bingo!

One of the last things I had to do at the end of my tour was to create two infantry companies out of the regiment and hand them over to the CO of 13th/18th Hussars for training prior to an emergency tour in Northern Ireland. An armoured regiment is much smaller than an infantry battalion, and two of the former are required to bring together four full companies. I was ordered to retain one operational tank squadron, a missile troop and my own headquarters, plus the remains of Headquarter Squadron. This seemed rather hard lines at the time, but it soon became a commonplace military operation, never mind the disruption to armoured training which came with it.

And so my farewell to the regiment included a two-day flying visit to Northern Ireland and a very brief glimpse of another world. Then quite suddenly I was about to leave a large slice of my life behind. In no time, it seems, the farewells were over, they tugged me out of the barracks in the staff car, and the youngest trooper presented me with my pennant in its frame.

It was down off cloud nine, and off to England with two overloaded cars, plus a van hired for the occasion with all the rest of our belongings. Sure enough, there was a buyer for the caravan - and we were gone.

CHAPTER XII

PUTTING DOWN ROOTS

Throughout our time in Germany, there had always been the thought of The Old Vicarage in the back of our minds. The Old Vic, as we called it, spelt stability and home - a real home. It was a tall, austere, red-brick piece of Victorian gothic, severe to look at from the outside, but with well-proportioned and gracious rooms within. A great door led into the spacious porch, and then four wide steps up into the hall. The hall stretched the best part of fifty feet, with a fine staircase leading up to the bedrooms. There was even an upstairs kitchen, to form the core of a granny flat. A breakfast room, kitchen, larder and bootroom lay 'below the salt' behind two baize doors leading off the hall. A flight of stairs led up from the breakfast room to the granny flat, and another flight down into a basement boiler room and wine store. There was even a church bell mounted on the roof, which I made sure could be worked from outside the front door.

The garden extended for something less than two acres, sloping uphill between two stands of trees. Four magnificent limes marched at the edge of a big lawn, which finished in two wide grass terraces. A small stream formed one boundary, fed by a spring somewhere up the hill. We were about 450 feet up at the foot of the Marlborough downs, and four miles from Wootton Bassett. About six miles away, Lyneham made its presence known with a continuous rumble from the RAF fleet of C130 Hercules transport aircraft.

We were just an hour from Downside, and thus we established a firm base for our boys to spend their teenage years. The plan was for me to join Barbara out hunting - a completely new experience for me - and we began to make contact with the Pony Club for the boys. Happily, there was a small stable among the outbuildings, and we took note that we were just inside the Beaufort country.

We were warmly welcomed by new friends, all of whom seemed to be farmers or doctors, with a sprinkling of retired people from industry and other professions. Most conveniently, my new appointment was at HQ Land Forces in Wilton, an easy hour by car through Devizes to Salisbury Plain. We looked forward to a total change of pace and occupation.

The first activity at home was to put a new roof onto the Old Vic. I had managed to beat down the purchase price because of the roof, which had allowed snowdrifts to form in the attic during a blizzard. It was good luck that the money saved was precisely the amount needed to pay for the roof. The attic was enormous, but inaccessible to anyone other than an acrobat, so we put that right too. Seen from above, the gables of the Old Vic formed a letter E, but we demolished the central horizontal bar of the E to form a U. We put a flat roof in the centre of the U, thus allowing more light to penetrate into the first-floor landing, and the hall below that, by means of a skylight. Moreover, we could now gain access to the rest of the roof (and the bell) without risking life and limb. We could get into the huge attic with relative ease, and then climb through a new door that opened onto the flat part of the roof. In theory we could sunbathe too, but Barbara made it quite clear that the garden would take priority. What fun it was, though, for the first time in our lives, to be able to play about with our own home.

Hunting was another completely new experience. Barbara found me a horse called Chieftain, a large Irish cob without too much promise, but big enough to carry me. I began to get fit for the saddle, and tried not to confuse the poor animal with the wrong signals. In truth, we needed to go to a meet and see what happened. We were in the Thursday country of the Beaufort, which arguably contained a greater variety of hazards than the other parts.

The Saturday country revolved around Badminton Park itself and, provided one avoided the famous horse trials course (as everyone did) we enjoyed the tremendous privilege of cantering in and about that magnificent estate. Every year when we go to enjoy the Badminton Horse Trials, I recall with pleasure the occasions when I washed off my horse in the lake close to the site of the fearsome and famous water obstacle. The obverse of the coin on a Saturday was the sheer size of the field, which numbered about 400. The Monday country was all stone walls high up in the Cotswolds, and the field seldom numbered more than 150. I found that easier to handle.

Back in the Thursday country the field was also much smaller, but the problems confronting the tyro were rather more daunting than a plain stone wall. I only have about a dozen outings to my credit, spread over two seasons, but I am told most people take ten years to get through the gamut of my experiences. Not many people ignore an order by the Master to leave the field and go home at once (it was not, I hasten to add, the Duke of Beaufort himself) - only to receive a letter of apology from the Master a week later in which he explained his concern was for my safety on the day. Too right.

Chieftain was feeling a bit sprightly that day, so we were well up behind a party of a dozen or so, hoping to stay close to hounds. The Master had got off his horse to open a gate, the while bitterly complaining that somebody else ought to be doing it, when Chieftain and I appeared on the scene. The rest of the party were politely and calmly waiting for the gate to be opened, and had formed a line abreast in perfect formation. I sought to join the line as right marker, but Chieftain carted me at speed in the direction of the Master. By some miracle I turned him left-handed, galloped hard across the front of the parade, and pointed him straight at an insurmountable, very thick and very tall hedge. Chieftain had to stop and we paused, chests heaving.

When I thought Chieftain had forgotten about his earlier impulses, I turned him back towards my interested companions. The result was not as intended. He did nought to sixty like a well-tuned Ferrari, and again I managed to turn him, charging recklessly in front of the stationary parade for a second time. On this occasion I sought to calm the fears anyone might have had for me by doffing my top hat as we went by. It showed form, I thought, and the spectators present much enjoyed themselves - except the Master. Ah well. But I have to say that, later that day, Chieftain gave me some of my best moments.

One of the best things about that time was that I came to understand hunting people, who represent the widest possible spectrum of society. Dukes and dustmen really do turn out together, and the common thread is an understanding of the countryside and its inhabitants, human or otherwise. I recall that the 10th Duke of Beaufort, who was still alive then, would never tolerate people jumping across land unless a fox was running. The communication between hunt and landowners was quite excellent, and the requirements of husbandry paramount. Protests by the self-styled 'animal rights' movement simply have no relevance.

Our boys were sixteen, fourteen and ten years old as spring turned to summer in 1972. In various ways they explored the world of the horse and the pony and, as a family, we began for the first time to develop an interest in Pony Club tetrathlon which was to stay with us for twenty years.

A tetrathlon competition takes a full weekend, embracing four events. The first is a shoot in somebody's barn, starting on Saturday morning, using air pistols of .177 calibre. Then the young are hauled off to a public swimming bath where the aim is to swim as far as possible in a given time. On the Sunday morning, there is a cross-country course for horse and rider of about a mile, with anything between sixteen and twenty jumps to negotiate. Finally, there is a cross-country run, to the accompaniment of much yelling and screaming from the mums. The whole thing is worked out on a points basis, and families become totally hooked on it.

In those early days we discovered that the VWH Hunt Branch of the Pony Club was closer to us than its sister in the Beaufort. Not only that, everyone else around us in the Thursday country had become pillars of the VWH Pony Club, and it seemed natural for us to go that way. We found that, in terms of tetrathlon, the VWH Pony Club were going through a time of relative decline after many past glories, and the enterprise needed plenty of tender loving care. Of all this there will be more to tell.

On arrival at UK Land Forces I discovered that, for the first time, I was to be given a job wholly removed from armoured fighting vehicles. I was to be concerned with the operational requirements of the Allied Mobile Force (Land), or AMF(L), which had a rapid-reaction role on the northern flank of NATO. This meant winter warfare training, much of it north of the Arctic Circle, involving both Royal Marine commandos and our own infantry in a series of NATO exercises conducted over difficult Norwegian terrain. The operational requirements were in a class of their own and quite fascinating to me.

The hardest nut, almost impossible to crack, was the problem of clothing. It was necessary to provide protection against the arctic cold, and at the same time protect the men from a possible chemical attack. Cold weather clothing consists of many layers of permeable material, allowing the skin to breathe and preventing sweat from turning to ice. Chemical protection is only feasible with impermeable clothing. At least a potential enemy would have the same problem, one felt.

The need for special 'compo' rations with an increased calorie content took me into an arcane world which trialled new and improved menus for the Services. I had been unaware that the Navy bore the tri-service responsibility for food, and of course they called it victualling instead. The palaver that went on to get a new menu cleared was amazing, following a very strict set of rules, and involving just about everybody to ensure that nobody got poisoned.

Langlauf skiing had to be learnt by the troops, and we had to look into the need for an improved bergen, and also a suitable sled or pulk, as they called it in Scandinavia. I met a most original inventor who, I think, came from Austria. He really had invented a way of packing a pair of skis into a briefcase. The trick lay in deciding precisely the two places where, along the length of a normal ski, it could be broken into three parts. The result was a short rear section, the central section where the ski boot fitted, and a longer front section. This inventor had designed a foolproof way of reconnecting the separate sections with a very clever spring-loaded device. He judged that, if a ski broke, the front section was the most likely part to fail, and he proposed that a couple of spares should be carried in a quiver on one's back. As I recall, he was targeting the ski-hire industry with his invention, and had made sure that his skis could be manufactured using the existing production methods of the mass market.

I promised him a free army trial under operational conditions, and a copy of the subsequent report for his own use, if he could get a set of skis to me by the following January, in time for winter training in Norway. He wanted money from me to help him set up a small plant in Leeds, and this I could not do. He tried to get an act together and failed. I often wonder what happened to him in the end. It was not just the skis. He had designed a bergen frame in such a way that, if two were fitted together, they formed a pulk. I really wanted him to succeed.

* * *

Linked to my involvement with arctic warfare was a wholly different activity concerning hovercraft. The Army had established 200 Hovercraft Trials Squadron, stationed on the Solent near Gosport after a period of trials in the Far East. The squadron was manned by the Royal Army Service Corps (RASC), as they then were, although it was never resolved whether one actually 'drove' or 'flew' a hovercraft.

The trouble with these machines, as people used to remark, is that they were a solution without a problem. That is to say, while they have the magnificent capability of sliding comfortably over rough or marshy terrain and then on to water, very few organizations around the world, civilian or military, have a place for them in their inventory.

One of the earliest successes was the cross-channel service which cornered about 25 per cent of the market. Another was the service to the Isle of Wight. But the numbers involved are seldom many, and the costs involved need careful analysis. Sometimes, a hydrofoil is preferred, as in San Francisco Bay, or Lago di Maggiore in Italy.

Quite specifically, the logistics of operations on the northern flank had led the Army to investigate the value or otherwise of hovercraft in that theatre. Movement through the mountainous terrain of Norway was pitifully slow, and the fiords offered a means of access for fast-moving hovercraft that could turn out to be crucial. My job was to study the squadron organization in detail, to observe the handling of the hovercraft squadron in theatre, and to begin preparation of a formal report.

It is interesting to note in passing that hovercraft were of no interest to ferry operators ploughing up and down the Norwegian fiords. Profits came from selling food and drink to passengers during, say, a two-and-a-half-hour journey, and *not* from selling tickets. There was no profit in a hovercraft which might reduce such a journey to about forty-five minutes.

For me, the hovercraft offered a wonderful excuse to dash off to the Solent at regular intervals. I even had a flying-cum-driving lesson one day when the tall ships were moored out in Spithead. This was hair-raising, for I seemed incapable of preventing the machine from sliding remorselessly sideways towards one or other of the great square-rigged sailing ships, and my instructor would have to take over to prevent disaster.

The hovercraft in question was the SRN6 Mark 2, similar to those which run to the Isle of Wight, and capable of lifting a platoon of men. A slightly different version could carry a landrover, or a few tonnes of stores. By the time I arrived at Wilton, a new trial had been planned which would take the squadron to a part of Norway north of the Arctic Circle. For ten days or so, the squadron was to be deployed between Narvik and Tromso, in and among the Lofoten Islands, in support of a major NATO exercise. I was to go with them. The time was September, and the autumn weather at its glorious best. We were at a latitude of 69 degrees, but the warmth of the Gulf Stream was effective even in those latitudes.

In due course, 200 Hovercraft Trials Squadron awarded 'Seaman Beardsworth' a plaque to commemorate his time with hovercraft XT657 during Exercise Strong Express. I cannot think of anything more easily or more joyfully earned. Not too many people can have enjoyed the privilege of exploring the reaches and sounds of northern Norway as we did, creaming along at a steady forty knots, scattering flocks of eider ducks in our path. We sped beneath beetling black and green cliffs that towered above us, the jagged skyline reflected miraculously in a calm, slate-grey sea.

Our base was a stony beach on one of the islands, and our ability to stop and hunker down in some hidden cove, unseen by passing 'enemy', was a revelation. Indeed, I found that the squadron was behaving in a way very similar to armoured reconnaissance, except that we moved on water and came ashore to hide. The hovercraft had two things going for it that had nothing to do with its logistic capability. One was a first-class radar, and the other was a powerful radio that appeared to be the only system capable of operating efficiently close to the mountainous terrain of the mainland. In consequence, the squadron was able to provide excellent intelligence information for the Force Commander.

This kind of thing was not within the ambit of the RASC, and I began to explain some of the drills and techniques involved. I can recall a period of about half an hour when the warrant officer in charge of the radar had sent a crucial series of radio messages to Force HQ without logging any of it down. I did the logging myself, and began Lesson One. The radar operator held the qualification of Master Mariner, and very good he was too. So was the pilot, and it was no fault of theirs that they had had little tactical experience in the way of reconnaissance.

On our return, I formed the opinion that the hovercraft was beginning to be a solution to several problems on the northern flank. But it is a matter of record that, in due time, the Ministry of Defence decided against bringing a hovercraft squadron into the Army.

I thoroughly enjoyed my time at Wilton, but my aspirations lay elsewhere in the equipment procurement world. I wanted to be a Project Manager (PM), and so it gave me great pleasure to be 'blown for' by my old boss Peter Tynan. I was to work for him as PM Future Main Battle Tank on promotion to Acting Colonel, with an office in St Christopher House in Southwark Street. It was the very job I had hoped for, and I could hardly wait.

CHAPTER XIII

AN ANGLO-GERMAN ENTERPRISE

For the next four years I lived in four different worlds. My office was in Southwark and, for most weekdays, I lodged in some comfort in South Kensington. A good 20 per cent of my professional life lay in Bonn, and I got back home at weekends. Family life became fractured, to say the least. There was much variety for me, of course, and Barbara had stability and the chance to absorb herself in a happy routine at the Old Vic.

But as time wore on we realized that we were beginning to pay a price. I had precious little time to enjoy my own home, whereas all the day-to-day responsibilities fell to Barbara, and these were poured out upon me every Friday evening at a time when I felt least responsive. What was worse, I never wanted to leave the Old Vic in holiday time, for I wanted to enjoy the place. This was most frustrating for the rest of the family.

We could not know that, in the end, we had to endure a full seven years of weekend commuting which by any standards is far too long. The effect of it all was greatly to increase the selfishness within me, to my lasting regret. In pursuing these separate lives, we were each driven back upon our own innate self-sufficiency, and it took a signal effort to restore that situation. It was another test of marriage which we could have done without.

And yet we still felt that our decision to set up home where we did was the right one. Neither of us could have stood London or any suburb as a permanent solution. We found much joy in our country environment, and the positive things outweighed the negative things for most of the time. My cautionary tale remains, though, for those who may come after.

Barbara and I adored my Kensington landlady. She was Mary Wilson, widow of a well-known amateur jockey called Boy Wilson who, at the age of fifty, led the Pathfinders into Arnhem before the airborne assault. The Parachute Regiment never failed to invite Mary to all their celebrations, and she always used to try and go. But she was getting on into her seventies, and saved most of her considerable energies for the business of going to the races.

This was not my scene at all, but I listened fascinated to her enthusiastic accounts of happy days spent with equally aged companions at one or other of the racing events. It seemed to me, although she never said so, that she was probably on nodding terms with Queen Mum, and in any case knew everybody else including most of the jockeys. The latter were crucial friends to have, for they gave her the final edge in her considerable knowledge of form. She always had a bet, and it was never more than two pounds. It is my belief that she made a steady income.

There was an occasion when Mary asked me how she should find a certain garage where her car would be serviced. It seemed that a relative had fixed for it to be done there at his expense. I was trying to explain where the big Hogarth roundabout was, on the way to the M4, when Mary slapped her knee. 'Of course,' she said. 'I know *exactly* where you mean. You go *left* for Sandown and *right* for Newbury!'

Mary lived in a spacious first-floor flat in Elvaston Place, between Queensgate and Gloucester Road. I was told about her by a regimental chum, Peter Tustin, who had also stayed with her. Mary enjoyed having a 'chap' from the Services as her part-time tenant, being at home with the language and the culture, as it were. For a ridiculously small rent I was given my own room and the run of the place.

There was a gracious, high-ceilinged drawing room with a balcony overlooking Elvaston Place, a long corridor leading past the bedrooms to a bathroom and, right at the far end round a sort of double bend, a neat little kitchen and a small dining room beyond. Thus my breakfast and, when I had learned how to cook it, my supper could be prepared and eaten in some seclusion. Mary's own sanctum was en suite, and there she would have breakfast in bed. In the evening, after a preliminary chat over her sherry and my gin, I would fetch her supper from the kitchen and settle her in front of the telly.

To begin with I used to find a friendly eating house in Gloucester Road for my supper. There were several options to choose from within easy walking distance. But as time went by I plucked up the courage to learn how to prepare my own simple supper, based upon the principle of heating up bags A and B in boiling water and eating the contents. I found this altogether more relaxing at the end of a long day.

From time to time it would make sense for me to drive the Mini up to London. There was a dedicated car park at St Christopher House where I worked, and I could park in Queensgate overnight without charge. The four-mile journey from Kensington to Southwark was simple enough and offered a welcome change of routine. The alternative, of course, was a trek from the tube station at Blackfriars, over the bridge and round into Southwark Street - alright if the weather was fine.

This whole arrangement was a godsend, knowing that I had a civilized lair waiting for me when the day was done. And then there were the two other worlds I had to inhabit.

The bulk of my time was spent in Southwark. From the start I found everything most exciting, in spite of having to work from St Christopher House. Along with almost all the many MOD buildings of that time, the interior was utterly depressing. My team was fortunate in being located on the tenth floor, though even then a clear view of St Paul's was blocked by the Bankside power station. Whenever possible one would go walkabout in the lunch hour, and by so doing uplifted the spirit as one gradually discovered the secrets that Southwark tends to hide under a bushel. There is much history there, and also some amazing contrasts. One could find Southwark cathedral, the old prison in Clink Street, the bustling Borough Market and the modern tower of Guy's Hospital, all jammed together.

Not far away is the old Anchor Inn, where they watched London burn across the river in 1666. Further upstream is the tiny house where Catherine of Aragon first spent a night in England and where, much later, Christopher Wren stayed while he built St Paul's, visible directly opposite. I was told that the Elephant and Castle emerged as the sixteenth-century cockney's version of the Infanta of Castile, and I firmly believe it. The variety of eating and drinking houses was enough to cater for every taste, and we tried most of them over the years.

Two hostelries deserve mention. One was called The Harrow, situated in an ugly street hemmed in by tall railway arches carrying trains to Cannon Street. The lounge bar there became an Officers' Mess, patronized by everyone from major general to major and their civil service peers. It was run by a retired mess staff sergeant called Albert who sometimes had a retired warrant officer of the Guards along to help. His wife Vi cooked excellent food, and a variety of beers were served by two attractive cousins. The Harrow was ten minutes walk away, and served the dual purpose of providing both relaxation and the chance to talk shop with people one would normally miss.

The other establishment was also ten minutes walk away but reserved for special occasions, perhaps for 'lunching out' a departing member of staff, or entertaining visiting delegations before putting them back on the plane. This was, and is, the famous Boot and Flogger - a wine bar of considerable repute hidden away behind another unprepossessing part of Southwark. The name needs explanation. The 'Boot' is a leather cup which used to be strapped to the leg below the knee. A bottle waiting to be corked was then inserted base first into the cup, and the 'Flogger' was a mallet with which the cork was banged home.

Before entering my fourth world, I should explain the background. We had been launched by our respective governments into a major attempt at collaboration between the British Army and the Bundeswehr. UK had the Chieftain tank, and Germany had the Leopard 1. We were to see if we could pave the way towards a single new tank for both armies. It was the view of the Secretary of State for Defence at that time, Lord Carrington, that it was 'ludicrous' for the four principal tank-producing nations of NATO - France, Germany, the States and ourselves - each to have a different tank. If there was to be a war, then it would be fought over the same terrain against a known enemy by allied armies, three of which served a unified command. It was perceived that a good first step would be for the Federal Republic and the United Kingdom to get an act together.

A note of caution came from the Chief of Defence Staff, Field Marshal Sir Michael Carver, who alerted the Secretary of State (SofS) to the dangers inherent in any compromise that might fall short of our fundamental operational requirements, thus undermining the tactical ability of the Royal Armoured Corps to fulfil its mission on the battlefield.

These things were debated during a major presentation to Lord

Carrington which happened only a few weeks after I had become Project Manager. My masters were hoping for a political initiative between SofS and his German opposite number to lay a firm foundation for our enterprise, and indeed to impart real impetus to it. Everybody who was anybody came to the presentation, beginning with Lord Carrington and his ministers, and on down the hierarchy until eventually they got to little me (I hid behind the screen).

The Chief of Defence Procurement (CDP), another of the senior mandarins in the MOD, was there as Head of the newly formed Procurement Executive (PE). With him was the Master General of the Ordnance (MGO) who, bearing a very ancient title once held by the great Duke of Wellington, held responsibility within the Army Board for the army equipment programme. Next on down was Major General John Allen, who had been Adjutant of the First during my time with them as a rookie. His title was Director General Fighting Vehicles and Engineering Equipment (DGFVE). Finally there was my immediate boss Brigadier Peter Tynan, Director of Projects for all armoured vehicles.

The other key guy was Mr David Cardwell, the Director of FVRDE at Chobham who, one day, would himself become CDP. John Allen and David Cardwell sought direction on how best to propose a division of responsibility for the development and manufacture of a new tank. Thus, it was apparent that both nations knew how to make good tanks, so how was work to be shared between two powerful industries? The presentation was designed to encourage the idea that Germany should be offered the hull, including the power train and the running gear, while the UK would retain the turret, including the main tank armament and fire control systems.

Lord Carrington made it clear that he was not yet ready to deal with the matter at the political level, but invited MGO to take up the initiative with his own opposite number along the lines proposed. This was a disappointment, but seen in hindsight SofS had been well advised. The truth of the matter was, as we came to learn, that UK was ill-prepared for work-sharing negotiations. All our ideas were on paper, as it were, and we had no appropriate hardware sufficiently advanced in development for us to demonstrate proof of performance to our German friends. Germany, on the other hand, had plenty of hardware to demonstrate at the outset because they had been laying the foundations for the replacement of Leopard 1 for some years.

In truth, although I never realised it until two or three years later, the occasion of the presentation to Lord Carrington kiboshed our chances of success before we had even got started. Someone very senior might have spotted the issue, and perhaps could have summoned the courage to recommend that collaboration be halted. I doubt whether Lord Carrington would have accepted such advice, on the grounds that the mould had to be broken somehow - I expect the Permanent Secretary or someone might have suggested 'knocking the generals' heads together' - which would have been pompous, but par for the course. While we never produced a collaborative tank, our enterprise was indeed successful in breaking the mould, and began a close association in thought, word and deed between the RAC and the Panzer Korps which continues today. The proof of the pudding lies in the fact that, many years later after we had all retired, the officers and men of the RAC would have been content to accept the Leopard 2 into British Army service if high-level decisions had ever gone that way. The same could not be said of the American Abrams or the French Leclerc, in my opinion. In any case, Challenger 2 beat them all, and the RAC are delighted with it.

And so to Bonn. It was extraordinary how blasé one became about such frequent air travel. Whether it was British Airways from Terminal One or Lufthansa from Terminal Two, one walked the route to the plane as though blindfold, with the minimum waste of time on the way. At Köln/Bonn airport, a minibus from the British Embassy would be waiting to take our little delegation to a temporary home somewhere in Bad Godesberg. Most of the time this was the Cäcilienhöhe, an Italian-run hotel high up above the western bank of the Rhine. Some of the younger ones wished they were not so far from the shops all the time, but no other establishment (and we tried them all) could compete with the spectacular view across the river to the Drakenfels. The Cäcilienhöhe had an excellent menu and, being well away from the sprawling town below, our costs were less.

Once a year, a letter would arrive from the green eyeshade brigade. It was felt that we should catch a bus from King's Cross to Luton and take a military charter flight to Düsseldorf. From there we should take a bus to the railway station and board a train for Bonn. Obviously, we would have to do the same coming back. Every year I silenced them by explaining that their solution would waste at least one full day and force us to spend one extra night in Germany.

I have to say that on one occasion our German chums had completely run through their travel budget for the year, and had to come over for an essential meeting at senior level by channel ferry. This was just affordable for them, in spite of having to spend a full week away from Bonn, but they drank the ferry dry - both ways.

We built up some very strong links with our German opposite numbers, and I have had a lasting friendship with Oberst Karl Pfeiffer ever since. Most of the time they would come to London and we would go to Bonn, but there were occasions when one or other of us had to demonstrate something in the field, making a pleasant change. There were three different committees at my level, and a Steering Group chaired on our side by the General (DGFVE). One committee dealt with operational requirements. A second dealt with administrative and contractual matters, and the frightful business of sorting out work sharing between the two national defence industries. The third committee met more often than the other two put together, and was known as the Evaluation Committee. To better understand its task, we should return to the negotiation undertaken by MGO on the orders of Lord Carrington.

In a word, the outcome was a lemon. The German side were *delighted* with our suggestion that they might manage the hull/chassis, but insisted that there should be a 'shoot-off' to decide about the gun. They had good reason to do so, for their 120mm smooth-bore tank gun was doing well (all other tank guns had a rifled bore) and the Germans were keen to demonstrate it to the world. The rifling in a gun barrel imparts spin to the emerging projectile, thus ensuring that it maintains an accurate flight path all the way to the target. A smooth-bore has no rifling, rather like a shotgun, and the ammunition has to be designed with integral fins, thus maintaining the stability and therefore the accuracy required of it.

It so happened that our own gun experts wanted us to try out a new 110mm design with a rifled barrel which they had been working on with an eye to the future. No one knew what it would do. And then in no time, the US Army became involved in the great shoot-out, for they had a third solution clamouring for demonstration against the others. Based upon the British 105mm gun that the Americans had bought from us some years earlier, they had developed new 105mm ammunition which was said to rival the armour penetration of 120mm ammunition, let alone 110mm.

Against the background of this imbroglio, the Evaluation Committee came into being. It had the unenviable task of working out a methodology to help everyone make decisions about which component parts should be fitted together into our joint tank design and whether, having done this, the tank was likely to meet our joint operational requirements. This meant doing war games according to agreed ground rules, and judging the results. It meant the creation of all manner of esoteric schemes for the awarding of points to competing solutions, and picking the winner.

Since nobody knew the answers, the embattled Evaluation Committee became the focus of considerable camaraderie as we wrestled with our task, and in truth became a focus also for much cultural activity. The usual routine, whether in Bonn or London, was to work through Tuesday and Thursday plus half of Wednesday, and sometimes Friday morning. Wednesday afternoon became 'sports afternoon' and provided the opportunity for relief from our difficulties. This took many forms.

It might be a visit to a castle on the Rhine, or to the Royal Academy to see the Chinese Exhibition. We would always try to entertain each other to one major meal. This might be at the Royal Naval College at Greenwich, or in some restaurant on the Rhine located in a chosen vineyard, where there would be a wine tasting. There was a memorable trip up the Rhine on an engineer barge belonging to the Bundeswehr, when we all had a go at steering the thing under strict tutelage. Vessels coming downstream seemed to approach us with the speed of a powerboat, so fast is the current there, and there was little room for error. What made it more exciting was the fact that one did not always pass each other on the same side, but switched depending on the particular stretch of the river we were on.

There was an occasion when, back in England, I wanted to take the delegations by bus to Hampton Court, and then finish the day at a suitable hostelry on the banks of the Thames. My specification was that we should be able to stand outside on a terrace and consume beer, while admiring a *pleasant* view. Then I wanted to go inside with a party of twenty or so and sit down to dinner.

I made reconnaissance one afternoon along the south bank, all the way from Walton-on-Thames to Westminster. There was absolutely nothing. I repeated the exercise along the north bank and, to my delight and considerable relief, found the London Apprentice, tucked away in Isleworth quite close to Syon Park. No wonder the rowing fraternity were patronizing the place, but what a sad reflection on our inability to exploit old Father Thames - *pace* the Seine.

We absolutely depended upon a most remarkable body of men and women. They were our simultaneous interpreters. One language would enter their ears and another would emerge, almost without pause, from their mouths. Unsurprisingly, they could only manage twenty minutes at a time. We all formed an enormous bond with them, founded on admiration for their skills, respect for their impartiality, and fondness for their sheer good humour. There would always be three - the home team would book two, and the visiting team would bring along just one. They were much in demand, and one had to plan well in advance to be sure they could match one's own dates.

The remarkable thing was their mastery of vocabulary and, of course, they could only specialize in just so many fields. Our demands were exceptional, for defence is always dealing at the leading edge of technology and some of the jargon we used was daunting, to say the least. Whenever we dealt with the mysteries of armoured protection, both sides wanted Karin Band, who was one of ours. She was Austrian born, I believe, and married to an English physicist. Her command was absolute and never faltered. Our German friends said that she produced classic German in a way that left no doubt over what was being said, and her 'instant' English had a wonderful flow to it. And then on more informal occasions she would say things like 'yes - he would like a shufti at that.'

Helmut was the principal German interpreter, and I only floored him once. I was in full flow when his incisive voice came into my earphones: 'I cannot translate "hell's bells!"' Thereafter I used to try and produce some awkward idiom when we were winding down at the end of a day, but he always coped.

As time went on, we began to understand each other's quirks and foibles. One thing that irritated us a lot was the length of time it took agreeing the formal Minutes with the Germans. So much time seemed to be wasted nitpicking over words, when the time could have been put to better use. We eventually found out why. For the Germans, the Minutes were a very serious matter, for they would land up on the desk of the Minister himself. I had no such worries. All I had to do, quite simply, was to brief my brigadier on the outcome and that would be that. So we learnt how to agree the content of the Minutes over a coffee or a beer in some private place, and the whole process speeded up.

Sometimes one side or the other would land up in the doghouse due to something that had greatly offended the other party. There was one most unfortunate occasion when the Steering Group had come together for a meeting in Bonn just after Remembrance Sunday. It was our turn in the doghouse, and Major General Mike Hogge was looking distinctly grey about the gills while his civilian opposite number pounded the table, rather to the embarrassment of some of my German chums. All of a sudden, a young German major at the end of the table rang a little bell, interrupting his leader in mid-flow.

'Gentlemen,' he said. 'It is the eleventh minute of the eleventh hour of the eleventh day of the eleventh month . . .' (Ah, we thought, of course – Remembrance) '. . . *und* so, ze carnival has begun in Köln!'

In a split second the scene was defused and we shouted with laughter. What was remarkable to us was the fact that his delegation leader knew nothing of the major's intentions, and we thought it a most commendable act of bravery. The major was promoted shortly afterwards.

What did we achieve? The great tank gun shoot-out took place at Shoeburyness and, as everyone had predicted, each of the three nations went away saying they preferred their own gun. From then on it became steadily more obvious that we would fail to determine a suitable work-sharing agreement. We tried hard, but the clincher in the end was the difference in our planning timescales. Our national plans for the replacement of tank fleets differed by some years.

It was in the field of Operational Requirements where we truly came together. The Germans taught us a lot about mobility, and we taught them a lot about armoured protection, to the extent that our ideas for a future tank concept became quite closely aligned.

More than all this, there were some hard lessons learned. It became crystal clear that successful collaboration would depend in the future upon energetic component development programmes. Concepts drawn out on paper were quite useless, as we found to our cost. One cannot bargain with paper.

Perhaps more fundamental than this was the realization that governments could not 'order' defence industries to collaborate and expect the enterprise automatically to succeed. Success depends on industry deciding for itself where its interests lie, and working out ways and means independently. Aircraft industries did just that post-war, recognizing that it would be the only way to survive. The result was the emergence of collaborative success stories like Jaguar and Tornado.

Governments have learnt how to define opportunities for potential collaborative projects, which must fulfil closely matched timescales in each customer nation, or be doomed to disaster. Consortia are invited to tender for the job, and their responses have to include an explanation of how the hardware is to be manufactured and introduced into service. Any successful consortium will almost certainly consist of an international team, who will have a work-sharing concept firmly in place.

So it was that our particular Anglo-German enterprise ran out of steam. At last, we all agreed that the project should be decently interred, and this was done by means of a pompous function called Symposium Alpha, which took place in what is now the Institute of Directors. It involved two sessions spread over three weeks and provided the opportunity for a senior wake. The photograph on my wall shows that everybody remotely connected with our endeavour turned up for the party. It was the end of a fascinating episode, and the beginning of a bilateral relationship that is still going strong.

Promotion to brigadier was on the cards, but not yet a reality. General Mike Hogge asked what I would like to do next, and I opted to go on the Senior Officers' War Course at the Royal Naval War College in Greenwich. This was duly fixed, and there began a marvellous five-month interlude of very great interest, no undue pressure, and the privilege of regular visits to the Painted Hall for meals. Greenwich really is a civilized place in which to enjoy a course.

Very senior people indeed came to speak to us. We got to visit both Houses of Parliament during debates, and to visit the Old Bailey during part of a murder trial. We clambered over Polaris submarines at Faslane and, in my own case, actually got to submerge in one of the smaller subs during Navy Week at Portsmouth. We visited Oslo and (a special delight for me) the far north of Norway where once I had swanned around in hovercraft. We visited Berlin for a memorable series of briefings and visits, and also Brussels where, by way of diversion, we had a private tour round the battlefield of Waterloo. We went to an RAF station where I got a trip in a Meteor and was sick. Then we went to St Mawgan whence the RAF fly their Nimrod maritime patrols. I never learn, because I volunteered for a trip in a Nimrod which I soon regretted. It turned out to be a training flight for pilots who were being put through their paces. This is not for the squeamish, and I had to be led away to the stern of the aircraft where I suffered in private for what seemed an eternity.

We were a happy tri-service bunch, with a civilian or two to lend tone, and our horizons were widened considerably for us by many distinguished people. For me, it meant a further spell of weekend commuting, remaining with Mary Wilson as a paying guest in Elvaston Place. But Barbara and I were able to enjoy a magnificent Ball in the Painted Hall to the sounds of a steel band that joined us, most romantically, on the dance floor. It was a very pleasant and relaxing time, with the opportunity to recharge batteries.

While there, I was told I would take over from Brigadier John Willis (who had become my boss after Peter Tynan) as Director of Projects with responsibility for all armoured vehicles. It was nice to know that John Willis would remain my boss as a major general. Not so nice to know that I would spend two or three more years in St Christopher House.

CHAPTER XIV

PROJECT DIRECTOR

By late 1977 the family scene had changed considerably. Both Barbara's parents and my own mother had died. Jonathan had celebrated his twenty-first the previous year and had opted for the Royal Tank Regiment by way of University College, London. James was twenty and had gone to work in a Knightsbridge winebar. Anthony was almost sixteen and still at Downside, wondering whether he had a vocation as a doctor.

After two patchy seasons of hunting, I decided to nail my colours to the game-shooting mast, through the medium of the College Shoot at Shrivenham which I had joined some years before. Barbara continued to hunt with the Beaufort, and we had both become involved, in one way or another, with the VWH Hunt Branch of the Pony Club.

Anthony was still into tetrathlon, and I had begun to help Brigadier Alastair Mitchell with the management of tetrathlon affairs. There came a time when I willingly gave up a week of summer leave each year in order to help out at Pony Club Camp. It was such great fun. With the permission of Earl Bathurst, the camp took place almost invariably in the stunning surroundings of Cirencester Park, with its huge woodlands and some spectacular views. We often took the tetrathlon bunch down to the private Bathurst swimming pool for practice, piling the boys and girls into our Rovers for a trip down to the private grounds surrounding the mansion. Everything else was organized in close proximity to the polo club pavilion.

The population of our own stables changed regularly. We had said goodbye with some relief to Chieftain, while Barbara continued to hunt a much-loved horse called Dumpy. For the boys there was Mr Spock, followed by Twink (who lived in the 'Twinklepen') and finally Annie, who gave James some great days out with hounds. An extremely aged little pony called Mr Brown came to spend some retirement years with us in a part of our garden. We put up a small shelter for him called Mr Brown's House, where he could hide from the prevailing wind. His special activity was to help with Riding for the Disabled, in this case with mentally-handicapped children. As for the other horses, when the time came to put them out to grass, we took them nearly four miles to a five-acre field we had bought near Wootton Bassett. There had been nothing closer in.

Further up from Mr Brown's little pasture was the upper part of our garden known as the Parson's Nose. This was a small plantation of Christmas trees, and the place where we kept chickens. The cock's name was Galahad, and the hens tried to ignore him.

We tore up an overgrown hedge that bordered our lawn and put in a clapboard fence and a shrub border designed by a professional. But Barbara worked wonders on all the rest, and our vicarage garden came into its own. I got as far as trying to create a herb garden, which was more or less alright, except the lovage wanted to take it over. I even built some steps out of cobblestones, leading down the bank from a wrought-iron gate in the hedge that fronted the lane. We were having a lot of fun and our roots were going in deep.

Back at St Christopher House I descended from the lofty heights of the tenth floor to the sixth, and lost the view of St Paul's completely. Not that I had many moments to look out at the vast brick edifice that is the Bankside power station. Life was busy. There were three different spheres of activity on the tank front, two of which concerned me directly.

Following the demise of our Anglo-German project, a new Project Team had been formed, under the personal leadership of Major General Peter Reid, to begin development of a new Main Battle Tank called MBT 80. The Navy had long since run their nuclear submarine business under a two-star chief executive, and the Army were glad to follow suit in the case of a tank requirement which had now become urgent.

Of concern to me in a sort of monitoring role was the flurry of activity on behalf of the Shah of Iran. He had ordered a tank to be produced for him in a timescale of less than five years. No test programme or trials were required. The Shah simply provided the funds and invited our experts to get on with it. A crack development team at Chobham had produced a design, and the Royal Ordnance Factory at Leeds was busy with the production line. The tank was to be called Shir Iran. My role, basically, was to ensure that British Army priorities were not prejudiced by this work, which had to be pursued with considerable urgency.

A third, time-consuming, programme lay in the capable hands of one of my own project managers, a contemporary of mine from the regiment, Alistair Mathieson. His was the unenviable task of digging into the elusive causes of some niggling reliability problems with the Chieftain tank. None of this was easy, for it was a matter of determining which of many key variables were contributing to the unreliability, and then developing a solution which worked without upsetting something else. We won in the end, but the RAC were getting a bit fed up.

All of this paled besides my remit concerning a programme to develop a Military Combat Vehicle (MCV) for the infantry called MCV 80. We had got to the stage when ministers had to approve the commitment of funds for full development and initial production. Various test rigs and mock-ups had been used to establish proof of performance, and high-risk items had been eliminated from the design. Costs were known, and all we needed was the go-ahead. This did not happen.

Dr Gilbert, the astute Minister of State for Procurement in the Labour Administration of the day, had drawn attention to the existence in service of the US Army's infantry fighting vehicle known as Bradley. Why, he wanted to know, did we not buy it off the shelf? Its performance appeared to match our operational requirements rather precisely. He ordered us to establish in full the implications of buying Bradley, against any competing arguments for continuing with our own MCV 80 as had been planned.

I did not regard this as an unpleasant duty. It would take me back to the USA and, more than this, I should meet up again with all my old friends in San Jose, for FMC happened to be the manufacturers of the Bradley vehicle. California here I come, I thought. The best bit about it was that I would have the opportunity to work out how, at long last, I could get Barbara to the States for a holiday. But first things first.

It is an unfortunate fact of life that, when dealing with armoured matters in the States, one is doomed to visiting Detroit. The people are fine, but the place is awful in my opinion. The best bit is the evening flight into Detroit over Lake Erie, with the setting sun glinting on the waters below. From then on, things deteriorate. Apart from 'downtown', the environs are featureless and flat. No one place distinguishes itself from another, and one is consigned to map-reading through a chessboard of roads until, with luck, one can identify the destination.

But in no time I was high-tailing to Detroit in search of Brigadier-General Stan Sheridan, who was the Project Manager for Bradley. There is a subtlety here, in the nomenclature of ranks. In the British Army, although a brigadier has one-star rank, he is not regarded as a general officer. He needs the second star (major general) for that. But other armies are different and identify one-star officers as brigadier-general. What is more, these officers are addressed as 'general' and, as a matter of form, British brigadiers receive the same courtesy. This is why brigadiers love to travel, enjoying '*Herr General*', or '*mon général*', or simply 'general' as in the States.

To return to our muttons, I found Stan Sheridan in Detroit, knowing I had to convince him that my mission was a real one indeed, and not a paper exercise for bureaucrats. He was an enormous help from start to finish, and began the process of leading me through the American Army procurement system, and introducing me and my team to the key players. His concern, of course, was to prevent this British exercise from upsetting his own priorities - rather like me with Shir Iran. We got on well, and I was delighted to discover in due course that his grandfather had been the Marshal of Tombstone.

Very soon I returned to my favourite city, San Francisco, after a gap of nearly twelve years. My friends fixed me up for a weekend in the Marines' Memorial Club, a stone's throw from Union Square and a short gasp up a very steep hill to the Fairmont Hotel. There I renewed my acquaintance with one of the finest urban vistas I know, and yet another dry martini. My reunion with old friends from FMC in San Jose was a generous and delightful affair, and I realized yet again that Service life goes on being exciting. One just has to be patient.

Having got our Bradley inquiry under way, I realized that it was now or never if I was going to get Barbara out to the States. My military business had helped to update me on the whereabouts of chums, and the possibilities for an extended private holiday. John and Barbara MacRostie were still in Los Gatos, near San Jose, determined never to move. Joe

Ameel had been posted to the Pentagon, and he and Betty were living in Alexandria, Virginia, just south of Washington DC. And Colin Eaton, an old chum from the Fifth Tanks, was serving as British Liaison Officer at Fort Knox, Kentucky. This was mightily significant, for Barbara and I had spotted that the next world championship horse trials (three-day event) were to be held near Lexington, Kentucky during 1978.

The plan was laid and we booked an 'indulgence flight' with the RAF. This was a marvellous system by which serving officers and their families could bid for spare seats in any of the routine flights that moved personnel around the world on duty. The catch was that there could be no guarantee of a place until the time came to board the aircraft. In practice, one received a call forty-eight hours ahead of the flight to confirm or deny the booking, and this usually held. In any case, one had to declare that funds existed to pay for a return flight by civil airline.

All was well, and we reported to RAF Brize Norton for our flight to Dulles International Airport outside Washington DC. The VC10 was crammed with people on postings to the Embassy or to various liaison jobs further on. There would have been several small parties concerned with defence business of one sort or another. I was to be a member of many such parties in the future, but it was nice to be fancy-free on this occasion.

Alcohol was banned - the cause of many formal protests in Whitehall (often from senior civil servants). Another feature of these RAF flights was that all our seats faced the rear of the plane, for safety reasons in case of a crash landing. We were told that civil airlines ignored this excellent practice because it was thought not to be 'commercial'. Rather like the first time seat belts became compulsory, or motorcyclists had to wear helmets. People found it difficult to accept these constraints on the grounds that they were 'not going to crash'.

I am glad to say we arrived safely at Dulles, to be met by the Ameels. Before the day was out, Barbara was getting a good look at the White House and, in the course of four or five days, saw and experienced most of what Washington and its environs had to offer. There are many contrasts. The centre was laid out in Napoleonic fashion by a Frenchman called Lafayette, and it is difficult for television to impart its magnificence. The scale and grandeur of the scene from Capitol Hill to Arlington Cemetery, embracing the Jefferson and Lincoln Memorials, the

Washington Monument, the Smithsonian Institution, the White House and, finally, the Potomac river have to be experienced on the ground. The National Air and Space Museum, a part of the Smithsonian, is an absolute must for a visit except, in our experience, for its appalling cafeteria.

But then, not far beyond elegant Georgetown, where Chain Bridge spans the Potomac, the scene is of white water flowing underneath, great woods descending to the river bank, and no inkling that one is still well within the limits of a great capital city. Similarly at Mount Vernon, the home of George and Martha Washington, now so magnificently preserved for posterity, it is difficult to perceive the twentieth century. Yet Mount Vernon is only fifteen miles or so from the White House.

Massachusetts Avenue runs north-west past the British Embassy towards the episcopalian Washington Cathedral, high above the city, and our friends the Ameels took us there during one of our driveabouts. They were quite flummoxed at my suggestion that we should then turn into the sprawling northern section of Washington. The residents there are almost wholly black American and represent by far the larger proportion of the urban populace. The Ameels had never been there before, and it amused us greatly that it should have been I who showed them the way. Our destination was the magnificent Roman Catholic basilica called The National Shrine of the Immaculate Conception, close to the Catholic university. Here was another contrast in a city of many colours, where Congress creates a life of its own, and the mayor tries to manage the rest.

The Ameels saw us off at Washington National Airport on a flight over the Allegheny Mountains to Louisville, Kentucky, where we were met by Colin and Judy Eaton. Fort Knox is a most disappointing place, like most military establishments. The bullion vault is a total anticlimax, perhaps deliberately so. There is an apocryphal story that a golfer on the course nearby once hooked a ball rather badly, and it landed on the wide expanse of grass in front of the vault. As he moved to retrieve it, a disembodied voice said, 'Leave it!' Well . . .

The Eatons were kindness itself, and so was a near neighbour of theirs, an American officer's wife whose husband was away on duty. With amazing but quite typical American generosity, she threw us the keys of her old jalopy and invited us to use it for our trips to the horse trials at Lexington. It is relevant to add that Lexington was 105 miles away. Each day we accomplished the round trip, and found that the rest of Kentucky was extremely good to look at, although it took a stretch of the imagination to recognize the 'blue grass' country.

The horse trials were brilliantly staged, but the weather was humid and stifling, with temperatures in the eighties, and therefore rather hard on horse and rider. We also had a major cloudburst, and a British entrepreneur did a roaring trade with plastic umbrellas and mackintoshes carrying a Union Jack motif. The US rider Bruce Davidson became the individual world champion for the second time in his long and distinguished career, this time on home ground (the first time was at Burghley in 1974). It was interesting to discover how few of the local Americans from Lexington itself knew anything about horse trials. The general approach was hey, what's going on here, we're new to this? That said, they entered into things with natural enthusiasm and many a loud whoop - even during the dressage.

This was a marvellous encounter with normal public life in America and Barbara quickly discovered, as we all do, how easy it was to go along with it all. One gets talking to complete strangers in no time. Mark you, the English accent catches the American ear very quickly, and then - where're yer from? - and away you go.

While we were based in Fort Knox, the RAF got a message to us saying there was no way we could have a return indulgence flight. Plan B came into operation, which was that we would fly with Freddie Laker from New York. I once heard a remark in Whitehall that Laker was 'a brigand'. Be that as it may, he transformed transatlantic travel for so many people by offering what amounted to a bus service.

Our host, Colin Eaton, went into action by saying that we were entitled to bid for accommodation in the guest house on Governor's Island in New York harbour. This was the US Coastguard Headquarters, just 400 yards or so off the point of Manhattan. We accepted with alacrity, and Colin fixed it.

It was time to fulfil my main aim of getting to California, and we bid farewell to Kentucky. Sure enough, Barbara marvelled over the mixture of mountain and desert scenery, and the final spectacular approach over the Sierra Nevada, the Diablo Range, and the Bay itself as we came to San Francisco. There is much romance in travel (when things go well) and we found it then.

It gave me enormous pleasure to take Barbara all over my old stamping ground from twelve years previously, and the family MacRostie did us proud when we got to San Jose and Los Gatos. At last I could share that part of the world with Barbara, and how much she loved it. It went by far too quickly.

Plan B loomed, introducing New York into our holiday as an unexpected extra. Governor's Island had its own ferry, leaving Manhattan every fifteen minutes (except in the small hours, when it became every half-hour). Moreover, it was free for coastguards and visitors like us. We landed up in a three-room suite, and enjoyed a very privileged view of both Manhattan and the Statue of Liberty.

But we were beginning to get the homing instinct and deliberately shortened our stay in New York. We climbed the Empire State building, visited the UN headquarters, and braved the metro in Times Square during rush hour. That was enough and we left Kennedy Airport by courtesy of Laker as soon as we could. To our surprise, we travelled in company with a near neighbour from our own village of Broad Town. Just another brush stoke on the canvas of life, one might say.

The issue of whether or not to buy Bradley was coming to a head in 1979, at a time when things were going very badly for the Shah of Iran. He was forced into exile by civil war, and the Shir Iran tank project collapsed as a consequence. The contractual and legal tangles which followed were not for me, but I became involved in another way. Egged on by the Treasury, the Army realized they could opt for a relatively cheap new tank by picking up the Iranian project and tweaking the performance specifications to suit our own operational requirements. Some years would pass before trials could be completed, but costs would be very much less than the proposed MBT 80. The latter was cancelled, and it fell to me to launch the development of what was to become the Challenger 1 tank.

Meanwhile the Bradley versus MCV 80 decision was bubbling and, in my view, the Challenger project began to have an influence upon it. I was particularly worried about the status of a certain supplier whose product would be required for Challenger. Unfortunately the collapse of the Iranian deal had left the company in a state approaching possible bankruptcy which, if it occurred, would leave Challenger without a vital component. What the supplier needed was a new contract fast, which a decision in favour of MCV 80 would ensure. The option of looking overseas for an alternative component would delay the introduction of Challenger into service, and increase the costs of the project unacceptably.

This, at least, became my view. Not everyone thought the same. In truth, the decision about Bradley was a real tough one to make. All those involved changed their view on the matter regularly - about once every week - me included. It turned out that cost was not a factor, unless the sterling/dollar exchange rate were to alter substantially. Moreover, the Vice Chief of the General Staff went on record to say that Bradley would meet his operational requirements. Such arguments as there were involved our own defence industrial base.

At the last, I felt we should stay with MCV 80. I am fairly sure my immediate boss thought differently. It was like that all the way up. In the end, the ministerial decision went in favour of MCV 80, which became the world-class vehicle known as Warrior. Warrior has since distinguished itself during the Gulf War and in Bosnia and, in hindsight, one can take the view that the decision against Bradley worked out very well.

By now I had no less than five Project Managers working for me as a result of cut-backs in the organization, and life was never boring. I enjoyed, too, our working relationship with the Germans, which continued seamlessly after our joint tank project had ended. Twice a year I would sit opposite my old friend Oberst Karl Pfeiffer to conduct much constructive business. A similar relationship was established with the French; and another with the Americans. One began to realize that 'the same faces' was not just a national phenomenon, but an international one as well. Most mistakes come from a failure in communication, and the four major tank-producing nations in NATO recognized the value of maintaining continuity and trust among old friends. The French thought this too, even though they kept at arms length politically from military affairs.

I was into my third year, and my relief had been nominated well in advance. The Bradley problem was still extant as we approached Christmas 1979, and I rang up my successor (who had a job in HQ UK Land Forces at Wilton) and told him that a visit to California in January was pretty essential as part of our handover. There was a silence at the other end apart from heavy breathing. Then Joe asked me to dictate the short speech he would have to make to his Commander-in-Chief to convince the latter that his trip should be authorized. No problem I said, and gave him the words. Magic.

So it was Santa Clara once again, where we spent two nights in a comfortable motel near the FMC plant. We learnt a lesson on the first evening about pizzas in America. The menu offered small, medium and large pizzas. We called for two medium ones. Each of these turned out to be the size of a small coffee table and, between us, we ate one only. We left the other as a tip. Beware the medium pizza.

While there had been an outside chance that I might be sent to the Embassy in Washington, it was not to be. But I was delighted to be told that I was to be Deputy Commandant at Shrivenham, and that my office would thus be less than twenty miles from my home. I was returning to my Alma Mater.

CHAPTER XV

ALMA MATER

For the first and only time in my service life I was given a company car. I delighted in my little black mini, which I drove daily over the Downs, below the Ridgeway and past Liddington Castle to Shrivenham. The arrangement was eminently sensible, for the alternative would have been a chauffeur-driven staff car. While the driver might have enjoyed the trip as much as I, there were many more important things for him to do. But for Barbara and I there came a marvellous feeling of independence which we had not experienced for seven years, since the days when I used to commute to Wilton from the Old Vic.

It was my fourth tour of duty at RMCS and obviously my last. It seemed that I might finish my service there. I settled once more into the world of military academe, and knew that I would enjoy the invigorating company of student staff officers. My responsibility was the running of the staff courses, testing the validity and quality of their content, overseeing the Directing Staff, and observing for myself the progress of the student officers. This last piece of duty was always a most rewarding experience and very good for morale. By definition they should have been good guys, and they were.

It was a time when the future, even the very existence, of the College was coming under scrutiny. This was not an isolated affair, but part of a much wider inquiry into the whole structure of officer training. The time taken up by the various inter-related activities contributing to the education and training of officers had increased over the years, representing too high a proportion of an officer's life. The curriculum for cadets at Sandhurst was always being looked at, but now we were all to be put under the microscope, even those who trod the hallowed halls of the Staff College at Camberley.

Broadly speaking, it was the sixteen years between the ages of twenty-one and thirty-seven that had to be looked at. A young officer would have to spend several months each on some form of 'special to arm' training (like gunnery or signals), and then a compulsory attendance at the Junior Division of the Staff College. Most officers wanted to do something extra when they became captains, like learning to fly a helicopter, or serving a tour in Oman. An alternative might be the achievement of a degree, or a year spent away on something like the Long Armour and Infantry Course at Bovington. Then came the crucial period of staff training, involving both Shrivenham and Camberley, taking anything from fifteen months to two years. Two tours of duty on the staff had to be added to all this, leaving precious little time for an officer to learn the ropes at regimental duty. To prove oneself worthy of command, it was important to achieve two years in command of a squadron, battery or company as a major. One year at this level of command was absolutely vital.

The sums did not really add up and, in consequence, there were very few selected for command at the early age of thirty-eight or so, which was what the Army Board wanted. Most of us lucky ones were selected when we were one or two years older. Hence the very critical look at time spent away from regimental duty. As an illustration, in the twenty years that had elapsed between my getting commissioned at Sandhurst and taking command of the 1st Royal Tank Regiment, I had spent only nine years at regimental duty. The warriors who had served during the War wagged their heads over this sort of thing, and quite rightly.

So it was that Brigadier Ted Killick came to Shrivenham to examine the raison d'etre of the College and its importance or otherwise in the scheme of things. Our defence, if that is the right expression, was to show that we 'added value'. The investment in the laboratories and the many training aids (from helicopters and missiles to guns and tanks) was significant and unique. The scope for research, not all of it with a defence bias, was excellent, encouraging a high standard of teaching among the academic staff running degree courses. The staff courses were supported by some of the best of the civilian lecturers, aided by a team of Directing Staff (DS) who had either just returned from commanding their regiments, or were soon to do so. An up-to-date feedback from the DS to the academic community was thus assured, being vital to the success of the staff courses.

Following from this dual capability of military university and staff college, there emerged a third role as an institute of technology providing a specialized service for defence needs worldwide. An example of this was a course dealing with the nuclear hardening of components, attracting many candidates from the defence industry. There were a number of post-graduate courses of varying duration, and courses in project management.

Our presentations to Ted Killick led us to the assertion that the quality of the Shrivenham product could only decline if, say, the enterprise were to be moved to a university as a whole or in part. This would have nothing to do with the quality and enthusiasm of university dons. Rather it would be a matter of failing to create an equivalent synergy to the mix of capabilities and resources which existed in the military environment at Shrivenham. Moreover, the effect on the staff courses would be fairly disastrous. The nature of these courses demanded a military venue where classified material could be simply handled, but their quality depended as much as anything else on the energies of academic staff engaged in the teaching of degrees, supported by research. To separate these would be to imperil the teaching of military technology unacceptably.

We won the day, but the writing was on the wall. Budgetary pressures were making inroads everywhere. A 'wind of change' was beginning to blow through defence with a vengeance, and the College remained vulnerable.

The problem was solved a year or two later following a piece of inspired thinking by the Commandant, Major General Dick Vincent. He saw that the only way forward towards the creation of an unchallenged 'centre of excellence' would be to put the whole academic function out to contract. Thus the dons could be brought to Shrivenham rather than the other way round. By putting the teaching effort onto a commercial basis, research funds could be sought from industry in a manner not open to civil servants. More money would attract more resources and increase the facilities. Competition would increase the quality of the academic staff themselves. It remained to be proven that a competition could be organized between interested parties, and that the MOD would save enough money by this means to make the effort worthwhile.

Indeed it was so, and matters were brought to a successful conclusion after I had left the College. Cranfield Institute of Technology won the contract, which has since been renewed after further competition. The College thrives with a much increased portfolio of courses, attracting many more students, and awarding its own Cranfield degrees. Most importantly, the Army continues to run it, and the RAF send their young officers there for degree training. One day, perhaps, the Royal Navy will also make full use of Shrivenham, and it will then become a true Defence Academy.

Extra-murally, I found it impossible to resist the temptation of doing a bit of amateur dramatics again, after a gap of more than ten years. This was to be a final fling, and I was cajoled into the hothouse of the One Act Festival. We entered a piece called *The Waiter*, and it was enormous fun because I was the waiter. We failed to win, but they gave me a minute little cup instead for providing entertainment. For a final final fling, I took part as the Reverend Chasuble in *The Importance Of Being Earnest*, and so gave up a hobby dedicated to the proposition that one must try not to embarrass one's friends.

And at home, after some years of involvement with pony club tetrathlon, I took over as organizer for the VWH. These things tend to go in cycles, and there had been a decline in interest for a year or two. A devoted lady (an international skier in her day) had been keeping it alive, and I had been helping her. I determined that we should get back into competition again, and take a team to Stoneleigh. So I began to get serious about the kind of training needed for my small, enthusiastic nucleus of boys and girls. To succeed, a whole family has to get involved in tetrathlon and, once they catch the bug, the effect is wholly rewarding. Fortunately, I had two such families to start with, and one or two other young hopefuls expressing interest.

Tetrathlon grew out of the perception that something other than riding was needed to attract the boys. Girls really looked after their ponies and loved them dearly. Boys, on the other hand, sought to gallop at will across country, returning to the stable with a sweating horse where there would be a willing ostler to whom one could throw the reins. This ostler (Mum) would then have to cool the horse down, groom it, feed and water it, and generally tuck it up for the night. Mucking out in the morning was not an option either. Hence the shooting, swimming and running elements were added to the riding. Of course, the girls took to the new regime like ducks to water, and really challenged the boys.

The facilities for shooting practice in winter were not good. We used air pistols against snap targets, the targets being exposed for four seconds each time. But one had to start by trying to achieve consistency with a static target first of all, and there were many disconsolate beginners who missed with five shots out of five. Having regard for the safety of cows, sheep and the like, we took our shooting practices to some strange venues. There was a huge hangar on the edge of South Cerney aerodrome where it was so cold that the mums went jogging round the interior perimeter, a good quarter of a mile. We visited an upper room in a pub to shoot at a tiny lead target about a foot square. On one memorable occasion, we tried to be accurate while shooting across the top of a midden with the wind blowing half a gale. The requirement was to get five good shots on each of two snap targets, and a possible was worth 1,000 points. My aim was to get them all to score at least 800 points.

Swimming practice had to be conducted in a proper 50-metre pool, and we used to hire one for an hour in the Cotswold Leisure Centre at Cirencester. The requirement was to swim as far as you could in a given time, usually for three minutes, but it was four minutes for the senior boys aged seventeen to twenty. We had a table to sort out the points earned, and I asked my lot to try for at least 600 in each of the swimming and running events. If you collected 1,000 points in either, you were very good.

Running was a matter of earning points against time taken over a distance of 1,500 metres. Senior boys, though, had to cope with 3,000 metres. I seldom practised their running except at annual camp, and left this to individual families to sort out. At a real competition, the shrieking mums were sufficient motivation.

The riding course was intended to be rather more than a mile involving sixteen to twenty jumps, and with standards varying according to age. It was supposed to be a straightforward hunter trials course rather than a tricky eventing course, but as standards soared over the years, the distinction began to disappear. A clear round within the optimum time was worth 1,200 points, with points lost for mistakes. I told them all to try for at least 1,000 points.

Keen mathematicians will realize that I was looking for a standard of

3,000 points, and children who achieved this target in competition received a simple bronze medal from me. It made a lot of sense, because in a team of four with three to count, three bronze medals meant they were into the rosettes. I set a higher standard of 3,500 points for a silver medal. Two of these and a bronze might give the team a win. Three silvers almost certainly would. The gold medal at 4,000 points put the young competitor in the running for an individual win.

This little scheme really caught on. By far the greatest pleasure for me was to note the expression of unalloyed joy on the face of a small person receiving their first bronze medal on a Sunday evening in summer as we gathered round the bonnet of my car.

During 1980, James was the first of our sons to get married. It happened that Sheila was to be supported by quite elderly grandparents, and so we suggested that we might host the wedding ourselves. This was gratefully accepted and the usual turmoil ensued. The Old Vicarage was ideally suited for a wedding, and our only problem, unsurprisingly, was the weather. Bride and grandfather trotted the four miles to Wootton Bassett in an open carriage, and collected a short, sharp shower on the way. They continued damp but undaunted, to be saluted in time-honoured fashion by the local policeman in the High Street.

I have considerable sympathy now for the fathers of daughters who are the more usual organizers of weddings. They are functions of considerable logistic complexity and daunting protocol, demanding the perception of a saint and the inspiration of a Leonardo.

There came a day in 1981 when I received a call from the Commandant's office. I went in to see Dick Vincent who looked at me quizzically and said:

'Simon, are you aware of what's been going on up in London?'

'No – I'm not sure what you mean. What's up?'

'Really? You haven't heard anything?'

'No!'

He came across to shake my hand and told me that I had been chosen as the next Deputy Master General of the Ordnance (DMGO) with promotion to major general. It is not often that I am rendered almost speechless. The post of DMGO had invariably been a second tour for someone of two-star rank, and here I was going straight into it. But there was no one else, you see, and so they came to me.

I had become a general officer - against the odds.

CHAPTER XVI

GENERAL OFFICER

I drove home in something of a daze, collecting champagne on the way, and remembering the number of times I had assured my family fan club that two stars were not for me. Anthony was home with us, and I surprised him and Barbara with glasses and a chilled bottle on the lawn. I have to say that Barbara showed all the symptoms of shell-shock. I am also fairly sure that she slipped away later for a little weep up in the Parson's Nose, believing that we were in for another three years of weekly commuting. I quickly assured her that this was not so, and that I planned to commute daily whenever possible. From time to time, of course, I would have to remain in London. Mary Wilson, my landlady for so many years, most generously allowed me to 'book in' to Elvaston Place on an ad hoc basis. Barbara cheered up at once, and we called for more champagne.

At about the same time, we came to the decision to move house into something smaller, coinciding more or less with my eventual retirement. We were determined to effect the change from big house to little house as early as possible. We would get the hassle over and done with - and *never* move again. When Jonathan heard this, his forceful remark was:

'You *can't* give up the Old Vic! I *relate* to this place!'

Tough, I said, but he had a point. The gaunt old pile had served us well, and even had a ghost - which only Barbara ever saw. This happened on three unrelated occasions, and featured a young woman in a bonnet and long flowing dress who walked through part of the garden chatting happily away to another, wholly invisible, person. The most memorable occurrence was when Barbara was able to shout a running commentary from upstairs while the rest of us gazed in vain at thin air - except for Connie, our old spaniel, who barked hysterically.

I always think the ability to see (or be aware of) ghosts is rather like the ability to go dowsing for water. There are energies around that not everyone can tap into. A ghost that shows itself is always seen to do the same thing, rather like an old video tape playing over and over. It seems to me quite wrong, and indeed presumptuous, to imagine that some sort of communication is involved. That way madness lies.

My Whitehall office was an elegant affair at the end of 'MGO's corridor' in the Main Building, with a very pleasant view over the Thames. The privilege that went with it was that I had returned to the central business of the Army. I was a member of a powerful two-star committee that dealt with routine policy before it got to the Army Board. I was a member of two Selection Boards dealing with promotions and appointments, and I held responsibility as the 'doyen' of the Weapons Staff.

Equipment procurement was not a direct concern of mine in the contractual sense. There were three two-star appointments concerned respectively with vehicle systems, gun systems and, lumped together, electronic devices and guided weapons. These three worked directly to MGO when accounting for the conduct of business in their field. I would come into the picture when submissions for programme funding had been given the nod by MGO. Then papers would have to be submitted upwards through the central Defence Staffs, with the aim of obtaining permission to proceed from an appropriate Authority. The greater the need for funding, the higher you went. MGO would become involved personally for the big stuff. This was a world I knew and understood very well, beginning with those early days when somebody had wanted to buy the wrong kind of compass and I had objected - without success.

Membership of the two-star committee brought a new and invigorating dimension into my life. It boasted the uninspiring acronym of SCAO (pronounced 'skoe') which stood for the equally uninspiring title of Standing Committee on Army Organisation. Everything other than operational matters (such as the Falklands) became our concern, from military music to the number of tanks in an armoured regiment. Indeed, the defence review initiated by John Nott called for a most detailed examination of our organizations, procedures and sacred cows. This was, by definition, the business of SCAO.

We considered the devoted body of chaplains and, with gritted teeth, asked ourselves why it was that they were in uniform. The alternative would be to rely on local parish priests, presumably some foreign ones as well, depending where troops were stationed. Then, in a crisis, these good men would be invited to charge off to some theatre of operations with the boys, 'leaving their sheep behind them'. The whole idea was crazy, but the guys in the Treasury pretended not to know and asked for evidence. It came from a chaplain who had been to the Falklands with the Welsh Guards.

'At the time of that awful disaster in Bluff Cove when the *Galahad* was attacked and caught fire,' he said, 'I found that I was able to be of some help to those dreadfully injured men because my face was well known to them. I was an old friend who had shared their service life. They could talk to me in an atmosphere of confidence and trust. I knew the language, as it were, having been a part of them. Had I not been there, I doubt that anyone else would have been - in the circumstances.' We rested our case.

But then we came to dogs. We discovered that the Military Police, the RAF Police, and our national police force all trained their dogs in different ways in different places, but for the same purpose. Measures were set in train to sort that one out.

After dogs, horses. We began with the premise that Her Majesty's Government sought to maintain the panoply of mounted escorts that supported State functions. If they did not, we reasoned, the Prime Minister would have to report to Buckingham Palace to explain herself. But suppose we were to privatise the Household Cavalry? This was the world of Bateman cartoons, but we commissioned a study. While we had no intention of suggesting the disbandment of the Life Guards and The Blues, we wanted to know what would happen if we were to rely on the open market for the provision of veterinary services, farriers, forage and the maintenance of a supply of black horses.

The figures were compelling, even surprising. The costs would have been astronomical, and the Prime Minister would have had a very sticky time indeed at the Palace. We consigned the topic to the archives with some relief and moved on.

Military music did not fare so well, in spite of our deeply felt conviction that it represented a national asset. Most communities scattered around the kingdom would have agreed with us. There were at least four teaching establishments supporting the three Services, including one for highland bands. We began to consider how to merge some or all of these. A long period of attrition began, and it was the size of the bands themselves which suffered in the first instance. There came a reduction in the number of musicians in each band by about a third. Later, the establishment of a band fell to the disastrous level of just sixteen musicians. A band could no longer provide 'military music' in the accepted sense, unless it joined forces with other bands. I once attended a function where a well-known infantry band attempted to beat retreat with sixteen men. I could have wept for them. Nowadays the total number of bands has been reduced still further, but they have been restored in size to an acceptable establishment of thirty-five. Mayors and others now have to compete quite vigorously for their services.

There were many wrestling matches of this kind following the defence review. They hurt at the time, but were small beer compared to the convulsions which have occurred since.

The work of the Selection Boards was the province of the Military Secretary (MS), representing the fairest and most comprehensive system for handling the Confidential Reports of officers that one could wish. Many chums in the Civil Service acknowledged this, but nothing ever got done to improve their own system, which was slow and cumbersome, often leaving posts unfilled for months.

Number One Board was simply the Army Board, and looked after the promotion and appointment of general officers. Number Two Board was concerned similarly with brigadiers and colonels. When in session, it consisted of five major generals drawn from a squad of about ten, supported by a brigadier from MS as secretary. Quite often MS himself would sit in, but had no power to intervene other than to offer advice.

The real donkey work came during week-long grading sessions. Our board room would be stacked high with officers' individual files containing all their Confidential Reports. Piles of ten files or so would be manoeuvred among us by supporting staff, and we set about grading each officer with marks out of ten. We each had our own system, and the key lay in maintaining consistency for what seemed endless hours. This was achieved through the watchfulness of the MS staff. The five separate gradings awarded to an officer had to lie within a span of no more than two marks. From time to time a discreet figure would appear by somebody's elbow inviting a fresh look. When this happened to me, I always discovered that I had been inconsistent in some way and could make a slight adjustment. Then MS would take the average of our gradings.

By this means a pecking order was established, and MS arranged the results in vertical columns by age groups. Halfway down each column was a red line, and promotions were normally selected from names above the line. However, it was a different group of five generals who sat down on a later occasion to decide about promotions. Yet another group of five would come together to make decisions on how to fill posts becoming vacant. For each post, MS 'ran' a list of eligible chaps and provided a personal profile on each. An officer would be selected after a considered debate, and the remainder would be rerun, either then or at a later Board, for consideration against other appointments.

Sometimes MS would draw our attention to the fact that Bloggs had been run for several appointments without being selected. We would consider his case very carefully, recognize his idiosyncrasies, and identify the sort of post for which he might be ideally suited. And so it went on. The system was utterly fair and foolproof, and must have eliminated wholly the vagaries of human nature, with all its vanities and prejudices.

Number Five Board was concerned specifically with appointments on the Weapons Staff, Number Two Board having first established the list of promotions. I was an ex officio member, and so was the civilian Director of the Royal Armament Research and Development Establishment (RARDE). Before each Board, I would have a briefing session with MS, and our discussions often had to look some way into the future. Much planning was needed to bring on officers with the right qualifications and experience for particular appointments.

On very rare occasions, I went back to Number Two Board with a recommendation that an officer be promoted from below the fateful red line. There would be a long debate, and MS would advise on the implications of taking such a step. The basic argument was that there was simply no one else to do the job under consideration. At the same time it was important to establish that, while the officer's grading was below the normal standard, he nevertheless had the necessary qualities to hold down the job without courting disaster. It was a rare event, but the few who were promoted in this way went on to do sterling work. It was

The author as Deputy Master General of the Ordnance (DMGO)

another example of the care and attention inherent in the system for dealing with an officer's career and the needs of the Service.

There was a particular difficulty when considering some of the senior posts in the Procurement Executive. These had been earmarked for rotation between military officers and civil servants. The difficulty arose quite simply because the civil service had no definable system for planning ahead - except when it concerned the career of a potential Permanent Secretary or Under Secretary. The chap I had to deal with in the civil service on these matters was an old friend from my days as a project manager. Charles Henn did his very best to kick his own system into life, and he usually managed to have a chap handy when it was his turn to supply, for example, a one-star project director.

There was another group known as Number Ten Board. It had nothing to do with promotions and appointments, for it was a social club. Membership was limited to some seven or so major generals in the Main Building, plus the brigadier who occupied the post of Director Public Relations. The purpose of this informal luncheon club was to talk shop once a fortnight in one or other of our offices over a light buffet. It was quite invaluable for finding out what was going on, especially during the Falklands operation, and happened every other Friday.

Attendance varied, of course, but we ran a strict rota for the provision of lunch. There was a mild rivalry between our personal assistants over the quality of the fare provided, and the existence of a small fridge in my office ('under test') helped things along quite a bit. We even managed strawberries and cream one day.

Another whole dimension to life was provided by the Proof and Experimental Establishments (P&EE) for which I was responsible, and also the Royal Ordnance Factories (ROFs) in my capacity as non-executive director on their Board. I had been many times to ROF (Leeds), where tanks were built, and quite often to ROF (Nottingham), where guns were forged. One of the most compelling sights was the master forger supervising the transformation of a giant brick of red hot steel into the recognisable shape of what would become a high-velocity tank gun of extraordinary accuracy.

As the months passed, I went to visit every one of the ROFs on an odyssey that took me all over the nation. I was shown quite fascinating industrial processes involving the creation and handling of high explosives, and nothing was more awesome than the world of 'the hill men' in ROF (Bishopton), just west of Glasgow. This was where they dealt with nitro-glycerine.

We all know that nitro-glycerine must not experience the slightest tremor. Its preparation in the laboratory calls for the transfer of chemicals from one piece of glass apparatus to another with some care. The industrial scenario of Bishopton called for the movement of material by automatic means from one machine to another. When I say machine, I mean the metal equivalent of a piece of glass apparatus, with lots of tubes and valves. In normal circumstances this movement of material would have been achieved by pumping the stuff around. Pumping is out for nitro-glycerine. This is where the 'hill' comes in.

There is a special hill at Bishopton, so arranged that the nasty stuff can fall under the influence of gravity from one machine to another. On the day I visited, production was not in process (perhaps deliberately) and so I came to see and understand more intimately the detail of the arrangements. As we climbed the hill it was evident that we all moved slowly, and spoke in low tones, even though nothing was toward. We came to the highest point and entered the command centre. There I found an impressive man who seemed carved out of granite, and it was he who controlled operations. He stood behind a large console and began to explain, quietly, how things were done. My eyes were drawn to a conspicuous knob, the only one painted in red.

'I imagine,' I whispered, 'that this is the panic button?'

Granite Man turned his head slowly and gave me a withering look.

'That, sir, is not a panic button. It is a Control Lever.'

The hill men of Bishopton were mightily phlegmatic, and might have qualified as astronauts given half a chance.

The P&EE were military establishments and, by the nature of their business, located mostly on some wild stretch of coast. The inmates revelled in their isolation, happy in the knowledge that visits by guys like me were rare indeed. Even the largest of them at Shoeburyness enjoyed a feeling of remoteness in spite of the apparent proximity to London. There was a fine Officers' Mess with a magnificent view over the Thames estuary, and even a little train of its own which, of course, I was allowed to drive. Away from the administrative buildings there stretched a wide area of coastal heathland with plenty of space to let off bangs and fire guns. It was a place where oil companies could buy time and space for the investigation of major conflagrations.

The real point about Shoeburyness was the way the receding tide exposed mile upon mile of hard sand every day. A new design of shell could be fired out to sea and, at low tide, lorries could be driven out to recover the undamaged shell for inspection.

There was another range at Eskmeals on the Cumberland coast with a long, safe template out to sea where ballistics could be studied using specialized radar. There was also an enclosed range for measuring the performance of high-velocity anti-tank rounds.

South again to Salisbury Plain and an establishment on the fringe of the Larkill gunnery range, near Lavington. The efficacy or otherwise of fuses was studied here in the most extraordinary and effective manner. A shell would be fired vertically upwards until eventually it turned over and fell back to earth. Clearly, good air traffic control and precise meteorological measurements were required before firing. They gave me a demonstration and predicted with uncanny accuracy the precise point of impact, which we observed from an elevated blockhouse. The point about all this was the nature of the chalk downland in those parts, which allowed the shells to burrow many feet on impact without damaging the fuses. They simply dug them out and had a look at them.

Another establishment made use of a stretch of the Pendine Sands in Dylan Thomas country. Here they had the means to test fire missiles by tethering them to a cradle which ran on rails. I visited all these places, much enjoying the accompanying environment while doing so, but they all knew that I was running my beady eye over their very existence, and the size of their respective organizations should they be allowed to continue. Each establishment impressed me with the unique set of circumstances that each possessed, and it was not easy to see how things could be done in another way.

One of my concerns was the Quality Assurance Directorate (Ordnance) - which was that part of an organization dedicated to maintaining quality in the products coming from industry into army service. Here again, reorganization on a massive scale was under consideration and would take time to unravel, long past my own tour of duty. In those days the Ministry maintained a quality 'presence' in factories all over the country, and the QAD men were given the necessary powers to reject components on the grounds of quality. As the years went by a new regime was introduced by which companies were made responsible for their own quality assurance under contract. This was a much more efficient way of doing things, and could be effectively monitored from the centre.

The QAD(Ord) Headquarters was in the Royal Arsenal, Woolwich and sported a number of listed buildings. They also ran a very fine apprentice school, as did many of the ROFs, and I took particular interest in them. Apprentice Masters were always on the lookout for appropriate engineering design projects as a training exercise in the final year. For example, at ROF (Leeds), apprentices had designed a wheelchair for a disabled boy who only had his chin and one thumb with which to pursue his hobby of photography. The completed product was delivered to much acclaim from the hospital staff concerned, not to mention that young lad.

This gave me an idea for solving the problems of target practice for our VWH tetrathlon enthusiasts. I wrote down the basic requirement, and then got out the Pony Club Tetrathlon Handbook to help me get the detailed specification right. I wanted four identical target stands made out of a metal framework four feet high. Each stand was to have two target holders made of metal, and joined in such a way that, when operated by a rope lanyard, both would turn away from the firer together. This would involve a spring mechanism, and the normal position of the target would be facing the firer.

There were two reasons for having four identical stands. First, I wanted the flexibility to set up two, four, six or eight targets. Secondly, the complete equipment would have to be lugged about all the time, and we needed man-portable bits of a sensible size. The final requirement, therefore, was that the stands could be simply joined together in the field, so that any number could be operated using the one lanyard.

Armed with my piece of paper, I showed it to the Director of QAD(Ord) and asked him if it was a fair project for the next apprentice design exercise. After due consultation, David Brighton came back to me to say that the whole idea had been received with some enthusiasm. It had the right ingredients for a successful project, and could be handled well within budget.

I was told some weeks later that the Apprentice Master was having difficulty in keeping the engineers out of the students' hair, for they all wanted to have a go at it. The final result was outstanding and fulfilled my wildest dreams. There was a formal handover ceremony, and I kept the apprentice designers informed of progress when we deployed the kit for Pony Club camp. Best of all, and I never knew whether this had been a deliberate feature of the design, the mild steel used for the target holders was such that it absorbed precisely the energy of the .177 pellets, and there was no ricochet. The squashed pellets simply dropped quietly into the lower shelf of the target holder. Brilliant.

Tetrathlon affairs were looking up, and we were taking part in competitions again with a number of individuals. The organizer of the Heythrop gang remarked that it was good to see the VWH back in contention, and then told me to be patient because it would take me five years to get a good team together. He was right.

I looked up one day from the preparation of a rather complicated paper concerning career patterns in the Procurement Executive to find MGO (General Sir Richard Vincent) standing at my elbow. His four-star opposite number from the US, a General Keith, was visiting the UK on duty and bringing his wife with him. Dick was hoping Barbara could help fill out a day for Mrs Keith in some way. This was much more interesting than my paper, and I accepted without consulting Barbara.

Fortunately all was well, and Barbara put a unique little programme together. The basic plan was to go to Windsor to meet a cousin of Barbara's, Dr John Clayton, and then go on to meet Major General Roy Dixon who had retired from the regiment to assume the appointment of Chapter Clerk for St George's Chapel. John Clayton looked after the medical needs of Eton School amongst many other things, and so the girls were given a conducted tour of Eton College Chapel as a starter. The subsequent tour of St George's was a real winner, and Mrs Keith found Roy Dixon's account of the Garter ceremony and all that went with it wholly absorbing.

Mrs Keith had a concern, and it was to do with the right kind of hat to wear for an afternoon in the royal box at Wimbledon. She was not really a hat person, and it was perhaps fortunate that Barbara was similarly inclined. The problem came to light while having elevenses in Kensington Palace with John Clayton's older brother Sam and his wife Lady Mary, who was a niece of the Queen Mother. Mary recommended a visit to the Queen Mother's own milliner, but the visit was unsatisfactory. So they went on for a somewhat gloomy session in Harrods, until Mrs Keith accepted Barbara's advice and wore a broad band of ribbon sporting a small posy of flowers. This was a success, and Barbara came away with numerous brownie points for her contribution to a pretty remarkable stay for Mrs Keith.

Not long after this, MGO allowed me to go on an official tour round the States, including a meeting with General Keith. I had a series of visits to make, taking in places that were old haunts, and others that were quite unfamiliar. Here was a golden opportunity to take Barbara back to the States again and planning got under way.

The key for Barbara was the generous hospitality of Alan and Marjorie Wheatcroft, who had been present on the occasion when we had announced our engagement. He was now a Brigadier serving in the British Embassy, and they lived in a Washington suburb. Once again the RAF got us to Dulles Airport, and one of my first duties was to call upon General Keith. Aside from more military matters, he issued an invitation to a party in his house on our last night before returning to UK.

The next stop for me was, of course, Detroit. I think I have said that there is no escaping that city, for it is where Tank Automotive Command, or TACOM, has its being. It was nice to be met by my personal escort officer, though, who made all the logistics melt away painlessly. I had an extremely good visit and received a small presentation from them. I began to realize that everyone knew I was soon to retire.

It was a Friday, and the next stop was San Francisco. I arrived about one hour before Barbara, Marjorie and Alan, who came in on a direct flight from Washington. One of our more efficient rendezvous, we thought. At some stage the MacRosties took charge and gave us a conducted tour of the Napa Valley where so many good Californian wines are grown. But there was an important reason for our visit to FMC, and this was the Multi-Launch Rocket System (MLRS) for which FMC provided the chassis, derived from the familiar Bradley vehicle. Alan was a gunner, and deeply interested in a weapon system which the

British Army were planning to buy. It was his job to watch over such matters for us.

On to Los Angeles, where the girls had a good look at Hollywood while Alan and I did another industrial visit. Then we said goodbye to Marjorie and Barbara, who caught a flight back to Washington while Alan and I launched ourselves across the deep south. We called in first at Fort Worth, Dallas to meet Vought Corporation, who were the prime contractors for the MLRS system. They in turn flew us across the stateline to Camden, Arkansas for a look around the factory where they assembled the rockets. Then back again, just in time to catch our connection from Fort Worth, Dallas to Orlando. It had been a long day, but suddenly, there was another guy from Martin Marietta, full of life and ready to entertain us to dinner in our hotel.

Martin Marietta were trying to capture our interest in an excellent 'smart' artillery shell known as Copperhead, and briefed us accordingly. Good as it was, there was no room for it in our budget, and besides, it was a first generation example of its kind. It is often wise to wait until the 'bugs' have been worked out of such systems. I am afraid my particular memory of that visit was my introduction to Fred. Fred was a fourteen-foot alligator whose home was the pond just outside the company canteen. Fortunately he was asleep when we met.

There was one more stop on the way back to Washington, at Missile Command, Huntsville, Alabama. Here we were entertained graciously by the military commander and his wife, and once more given a series of high-class presentations. Then we were flown to Atlanta, and caught a flight to Washington National Airport. Landing there was always a special experience for the passengers, as the aircraft weaved to follow a line above the bends of the Potomac River, giving us a sensational view towards the Capitol over the Lincoln Memorial, before skimming over Fourteenth Street Bridge onto the runway.

We just had time to change at the Wheatcroft's house before we all departed for the party with General and Mrs Keith. They lived in one of the large, spacious quarters on the banks of the Potomac reserved for guys with four stars. It was a very elegant house, and we much enjoyed reminiscences with Mrs Keith about her own unique trip to England. As we left their home at about nine o'clock, the snow began to fall.

We woke the following morning to a white-out, with the snow some eighteen inches deep. This does not happen often in Washington, but when it does, the capital comes to a grinding halt. Too late, the Government advised people not to come in to work. Very many frustrated souls took ten hours or so to turn round and get back home. I know that Stan Sheridan, then a major general and working in Washington, had the good sense to stay at home and enjoy the day off. Much of the problem was to do with the automatic gearboxes and fluid flywheels which were standard in American cars. They could not cope with the snow, especially on some of the quite steep hills in the city.

Alan Wheatcroft had the answer, which was fortunate because we had an appointment with an Assistant Secretary of Defence in the Pentagon. I had a point or two to make with him on behalf of MGO, and we needed to keep our date. Alan had a second car in the form of a battered old Mercedes with a crash gearbox and chains to fit to the wheels. We enjoyed a steady progress through Washington, hampered only by the many stranded cars littering every thoroughfare. We kept our date with the politician, for he too had made sure that he would reach the Pentagon - probably by helicopter. We returned in triumph to the Embassy, dodging the many obstacles that had skidded to a halt in Massachusetts Avenue.

We soon learnt that the RAF flight from Dulles would be delayed twenty-four hours, and we needed only to return to the Wheatcroft home to enjoy an unexpected extra evening together. On arrival at the foot of the hilly residential street in which they lived, we discovered that further progress was impossible, even with chains. Snowploughs had cleared a single track along the main drag, and if we were to park the car there, we needed a lay-by in which to put it. We spotted a small snowplough nearby, apparently owned and worked by a private individual who had seized the opportunity for an extra dollar. Dressed in my general's uniform, which must have looked to him like something out of Ruritania, I ran across and did a deal with him for ten dollars. He carved us out a lovely lay-by, used later by many other residents. Then Alan led the way, knee deep, towards his house and a warm welcome from our womenfolk.

We took off on time the next day to conclude another hectic but enjoyable dose of American life.

* * *

There is the familiar saying that old soldiers never die, they simply fade away. This can be very true for the Whitehall warrior, and many senior officers elsewhere, who land up at the age of fifty-five or more to retire far away from the regimental scene. My own last year was a happy one in this regard, not least because Jonathan was now Adjutant of the First, and because the regiment was stationed, as luck would have it, at Bovington and Lulworth.

First, though, there came an invitation to us both from a colleague of mine on SCAO to join him for a ceremony of Beating the Retreat by the Light Infantry. The venue was the Royal Crescent in Bath and we were to enjoy an exceptional evening. We came to learn that, for occasions of this sort, the local residents who happened to be at home would put out all their lights and substitute them with a single candle in each window. The effect was magical as dusk descended, enhanced still further by two spotlighted buglers high up on the roof at each corner. This was lump-in-the-throat stuff.

Barbara and I enjoyed three other splendid occasions of pomp and circumstance. We took ourselves to Wembley to see a Festival of Massed Bands - 2,000 musicians in all - which was a truly stirring affair. We got tickets for Trooping the Colour, because everyone has to be there at least once in their lives, and the weather smiled upon us all. And there was a happy morning at the Palace.

To our considerable delight Barbara and I were invited by Jonathan to a Ladies' Night Dinner at Lulworth, where we met all kinds of friends. Last of all, I was dined out by my regiment in traditional style, and I felt that I had indeed come home again.

CHAPTER XVII

GAMEKEEPER TURNED POACHER

Everything started happening at once in the late summer of 1984. I left the Army officially on 14 September, but by then I was already picking up drumbeats from an unexpected quarter about my possible future employment. Equally unexpected was a firm proposal from a cavalry colleague about buying the Old Vicarage. This was Brigadier Roland Notley, who had once served on my project management team. Fortunately Barbara and I had spotted our future home, up for sale some ten miles away, with possession in early December. But Roland put us out on the street in late September, so we had to pig it for eleven weeks in a quite ghastly little holiday cottage that was virtually uninhabitable outside high summer. This was in a neighbouring village called Bushton.

Meanwhile, Jonathan was about to get married to Ginnie on 29 September. Her home was in Kent, and the great event was a welcome and civilized relief from the tribulations of our temporary abode. On top of all this, and to my great amazement, I was off to the States with my new employer for a three-day trip to Washington in the first week of October. Life was like a firework display, with 'oohs' and 'aahs' every other minute.

Emptying the Old Vic of our worldly goods was a nightmare. We could only live out of suitcases in Bushton, so there was no alternative to putting most of our stuff into store. That is to say, everything that had not been thrown into a skip at the bottom of our short drive (daughter-in-law Sheila spent much time upended in the skip, 'rescuing' a few items for herself and James).

We made an exception over some rather special bits of furniture and a few paintings, which we ferried about in our horse-trailer for distribution among the garages and barns of kind friends. And we made life more difficult for ourselves by deciding to take away two staddle-stones from the garden. These are very heavy things, but it was worth the effort. We had to find temporary homes for the horses and the chickens, of course. The dogs, as one might imagine, went into a serious decline, maintaining lugubrious sentry duty at the front door. The cat ignored it all, as cats do.

We moved into our new home on 4 December. It was called Granville House, a quite unsuitable and pretentious name for a cottage, we thought. Barbara had the brilliant idea of calling it Meerhay, after Meerhay Manor in Beaminster where I had proposed to her, also on 4 December. We asked around the village and nobody seemed to mind, so Meerhay it became.

Within six months or so we had added an extension to make an L shape, and reorganized the interior. We now had a large drawing room, a large square kitchen-cum-dining room, and three double bedrooms. There was a hall, a study for me and a laundry room. We were surrounded, as the title deeds had it, with 'five acres, one rood, and twenty five perches or thereabouts'. The garage was misused to form a store for old Victorian tallboys, unwanted beds and much else from the Old Vic. This meant that our cars stayed out in the open for at least eighteen months, until Barbara became stern and dragooned the family into dividing the spoils.

Horses, chickens and dogs were soon settled - but the cat chose to sulk for a week, as cats do. There is an interesting statistic to record. Bearing in mind, first, that Barbara had to spend a couple of months with her parents on three occasions in default of a quarter to live in; and secondly, that we had actually lived in the Old Vic for the lengthy period of twelve and a half years; then Meerhay became the thirty-second home for Barbara to lay her head in during thirty-one years of marriage. It is not an unusual statistic from Service life in those days.

Two days after Jonathan's and Ginnie's wedding I became a part-time employee of Oceonics Defence, whom nobody had ever heard of. What is Simon doing? they said. In fact, Oceonics had only just decided to expand into defence by buying up five small companies. Between them these companies handled a number of world-class technologies, and my brief was going to be the marketing abroad of the suspension technology fitted to the Challenger tank. Oceonics' normal business was connected to the offshore oil industry, and they needed to bring in some knowledgeable people to handle their defence interests for them.

David Wright, who can be called a captain of industry these days, was the chief executive, and it was he who hired me. The chairman was Fred East, a distinguished ex-director of the Royal Armament Research and Development Establishment and, at that time, a consultant to the Cabinet Office. No sooner had I arrived than David whisked me off to Washington to decide between two candidate consultancy firms who might assist us in the States. My second career had begun in style, and I much enjoyed my introduction to the privileges of club-class travel.

Our offices were close to Centre Point in Charing Cross Road, and the downside to an otherwise exciting life was my enforced use of Tottenham Court Road tube station on my way to and from Paddington. I would work three or four days a week, and regularly took to the air on business. My principal brief was in the States, but there were other trips to places like Zurich, Bolzano and Stuttgart. It was during these early days that, for the first and only time in my life, I drove at a sustained speed of 105 miles per hour on the autobahn north of Basel.

In the States, it was my pleasure to work with an old friend called Howard ('Knobby') Glock, a retired colonel from the US Army. He was the project officer assigned to us by RBI Inc, the firm of consultants whom we had hired in Washington. We had had many official dealings together on highly sensitive matters and knew each other well. Wherever I went in the States, Knobby would come too and 'open doors' for me.

After a month or two, Oceonics rationalized the work of their defence companies, and it was on behalf of Air-Log Ltd that I worked on the marketing of suspension technology. The technology itself lay in the hands of two design engineers, John Woollard and John Harris, who became good friends of mine. But while Air-Log had its being in Aldershot, we three continued to operate from London.

The first big trip to the States and to Canada lasted two weeks, and the travel budget could only afford one engineer to support me. I forget how it was decided that the lot should fall upon John Woollard, but from that moment John Harris made it abundantly clear that it was to be him the next time. Neither had crossed the Atlantic before, and I took great pleasure in serving as tour guide for both of them over the coming months.

Woollard and I set off in May 1985 for a lengthy trip that began in Canada. The pattern was pretty much the same each time we travelled. On this occasion, we went to Ottawa to visit Defence HQ, and then Toronto and London (Ontario) to make presentations to a couple of firms, before ending the week in Washington DC. We remained for five nights, embracing the weekend and two days of briefings at the Embassy and with RBI Inc. The rest of that week took us to York (Pennsylvania), the compulsory visit to Detroit, and the even more compulsory trip to San Francisco for the second weekend. The first two days of the following week took us to San Jose and to Seattle, before we flew home direct from San Francisco.

There were four more excursions in the course of the next twelve months, visiting many new places as we searched for a possible teaming partner for Air-Log. Sometimes we had to travel with 'rinky-dink' airlines, as Knobby called them. There were some memorable moments with these on at least three occasions. The most startling was on a trip from Chicago to Buffalo (New York). The pilot began by saying that we had some 'weather' up ahead, and that he was planning to climb above it. We began to get thrown about a bit after a while, and the pilot came up with: 'So-o we didn't get above it, folks! Fasten seat belts and we'll ride it out.'

We endured an extremely turbulent approach towards the airport, until we were not much more than 100 feet above the ground. At this point the aircraft tilted sharply to the right, the wing pointing almost vertically downwards. Somehow the pilot got us down safely. As we approached the gangway, he gasped in his lilting southern accent: 'We-ell, folks, ahm sure glad to be on the gro-ound, and ah hopes you are tew!'

There came a time when it seemed that the big agricultural manufacturer John Deere might contemplate a relationship with Air-Log. This did not happen, but our preliminary dealings with them took us to a place on the banks of the Mississippi where four towns called Moline, Rock Island, Davenport and Bettendorf constituted the unromantic-sounding Quad Cities. It was my only experience of the mid-west, and I began to understand my Washington friends who had said, 'you won't find any city slickers out there'. Be that as it may, John Deere enjoyed one of the most imaginative headquarters buildings I have ever visited (designed by a Scandinavian architect) and they were charming people to deal with.

At about this time, Oceonics sold their defence interests to a company called Adwest, realizing that the business was not for them. Air-Log expanded under their new masters, but rationalized their affairs by moving out of several expensive London buildings, including the one in Charing Cross Road. My place of work became Aldershot, at about the same time that we ceased to pursue our interests in the States. I spent an increasingly irksome year commuting by car the seventy miles to Aldershot.

Fortunately, some other irons were being poked into the fire. At about the time I left the Service in late 1984, Perkins Engines of Peterborough had decided to make a serious move into the defence market. They were well established as manufacturers and suppliers of diesel engines worldwide, and in consequence many of their commercial diesels were already in use in military forklift trucks and engineer plant of all kinds. This was a profitable but low profile business.

Their decision to buy the Rolls Royce Military Diesel Division in Shrewsbury, however, brought them into the high profile world of tanks and cross-country mobility. The fighting vehicle propulsion business is very different to the commercial scene, which calls for diesel engines to be turned out in many tens of thousands for fitment, typically, into lorry fleets. A commercial order had to be responded to in a matter of weeks, whereas the timescale for the delivery of a military power pack could be measured in years. This was because it had to conform to the procurement programme of the vehicle for which it was intended.

It took Perkins two years to understand fully the nature of this new business, and just how well placed they were to meet its challenges. Then they came looking for me, with a proposal that I should serve as their military consultant. This was just the sort of job I had been hoping for, and I asked Air-Log if they, too, would enlist me as a consultant rather than as a part-time employee. Letters of Appointment were exchanged, and I began my third career on 1 April 1987.

Much had been happening on the home front. Anthony married Suzie in July 1985, and they settled in Camberwell Green to complete their medical studies. Six months later, Jonathan began his first year on the staff course at Shrivenham, and then went on to Camberley for the second year. James remained hard at work in the estate agency business, with a house in Wootton Bassett.

In the summer of 1985 I had the courage to run our own two-day tetrathlon event for the rest of the Pony Club branches in what was called Area Nine. For the first time I understood what it was like facing up to Mum - protesting, perhaps, over my decision that Polly's shot had *not* clipped the bull - or claiming that Bobby had swum a metre more than the distance recorded by the Lane Judge. But we got away with it and, to my dismay, I was required the following year to run the Area Nine Competition. The winning teams and individuals would be entered for the Pony Club Championships at Stoneleigh, so it was serious stuff. I even had an Official Steward breathing down my neck. My team of helpers were magnificent, and we were invited to run the Area Competition again in 1987. We began to feel that the VWH were making up for their temporary absence in previous years. Even better was the satisfaction that some of our own young people were getting to Stoneleigh. Area Nine was very strong in tetrathlon in those days, and to win a team or individual competition in any of the Area events was no mean achievement. Tetrathlon families would attend seven or eight events in the course of the summer, apart from Stoneleigh, and life was full.

Another event in the summer of 1985 was our trip to Germany to attend the Presentation of Standards by the Queen at a ceremony near Paderborn. Her Majesty is our Colonel-in-Chief but, being the monarch, her presence among us is a relatively rare event. As it happened, we were extremely lucky to have the Queen visit us again only eighteen months later for dinner with the officers in the Vintner's Hall.

But we swarmed across the Channel for the Standards Parade, and enjoyed a spectacular day. There is something hugely impressive about four regiments of tanks spread before one, all starting their engines together some three hundred yards away, and then crawling thunderously forwards to a mounting crescendo of 'Chariots of Fire'. You know then why it was that you joined, and you tend to become speechless.

My little Welsh springer Connie was a dog of character. We are used to eccentric dogs on our shoot, and Connie's claim to fame was to be the only dog which buried a pheasant. In truth, her mouth was a bit too small for retrieving, and she rightly gave priority to the hunting out of birds. But on this day she picked up a hen pheasant for me and started back. I encouraged her noisily, but she noticed that all manner of birds were flying about and that her presence was required elsewhere. So she deposited the bird and used her nose to cover it with fallen leaves before trotting off on more important business.

In March 1986 she gave birth to a magnificent litter of seven bitches. Five days later my diary records: 'Megan surviving - so far'. Connie was incapable of mothering. She was ensconced in a wooden nursing box packed with shredded paper from the stable. The squeaking of her puppies was an annoyance for her and she tried to bury them under pieces of paper. Too late we realized what was happening and we found two corpses in the morning. I took the dreadful decision to kill three more of the puppies, and Barbara and I set about trying to keep the remaining two alive. We succeeded only with Megan, who is now in her twelfth year and extremely fit - not to say hysterical on occasion - but perhaps we could expect her to be just a little neurotic.

My new life as a self-employed consultant gave me plenty of work. I recall a time when I had about six clients on my books, but it was more usually three. There was a lot to do on behalf of Perkins in the way of raising their profile around the MOD, bringing the military decision-makers to visit their factories and encouraging a series of formal presentations in London. I began to renew many friendships among my old colleagues, quite often keeping myself up to date by allowing them to talk over lunch. What industry needed to know were the likely prospects for business, in what quantity, and in what timescale. Then they could decide, first, whether to participate in a new equipment programme, and secondly, how best to prepare for the almost inevitable competition which followed.

My concern always was to ensure that my chums in industry took every opportunity to instil in their potential customers an abiding confidence in the ability of their Company to provide a quality product on time and within the budget. Personalities had to meet as often as possible, amicable debate had to be encouraged on the more difficult issues, and a first-hand knowledge of a firm's skills and capabilities imparted to all the key players.

More than this, I was able to help by interpreting the thoughts of 'the

The author on a shoot at Shrivenham

user' on matters of policy, organization, tactics and funding. As somebody once said, 'They'll say more to Simon than they will to us.' It was an important function to fulfil, and I often found myself calming people down after they had frightened themselves by trying to read the entrails.

When asked what differences I had discovered in the industrial world, I would usually reply that the profit motive was an all-embracing factor that did not impinge in normal service life. We all knew this, of course, but to see and hear it in operation at first hand could be startling. Officers and men are trained to sort problems out, to get things going again, and to keep on until the job is done. The cost in effort and resource is justified for operational reasons. In industry, a line of business could be abandoned very quickly if a hard-headed Board saw little profit in it. It is the job of a managing director to demand, all the time, whether it is worth the candle to stay in the defence business. Hence the constant examination of entrails by marketing people, and its stressful consequences.

On the other hand, once a company was placed under contract, then the effort and hard work devoted to ensuring a successful outcome often matched anything I had ever seen in the Services. This was the profit motive working again, of course, but also a determination to do well for the company. In that sense, the commitment and drive comes from a motivation that a soldier would recognize.

I often found that, in the face of some contentious issue, senior management would develop a head of steam behind the idea that a Minister should be confronted immediately. I always counselled against this. Almost always, an initiative of that kind would be doomed to go off at half-cock. A Minister needs to be briefed first, and the timing of a visit to his office orchestrated with the cooperation of his staff. In this way the busy Minister will be able to respond with knowledge and understanding to the points being made by the managing director. The alternative, should he not be briefed, is that he will listen politely but unhelpfully, and afterwards require his staff to drop everything and find a few answers for him. This infuriates everybody and loses brownie points for the managing director. And momentum is lost.

Another difference I found in industry is that people seldom teach others to do *their* job. In the Army we are used to seconds-in-command to whom we continually give the opportunity to practise command themselves. Industry is good at training young managers and supervisors in all aspects of the company's business, but I have never heard of a junior deputizing at a Board meeting. The opportunity for advancement seems to rest unduly on the need to try for a higher-paid job in another firm.

My own way of life was a busy one, with lots of authority and relatively little responsibility, most of the time at a pace of my choosing. I spent much time in London, Aldershot, Peterborough and Shrewsbury, and in the process began to feel that I was close to the Army again.

Among the family, we had begun to visit France for a summer break each year in different groupings. Jonathan's in-laws (we called each other outlaws) owned a group of farm buildings in the Charente Maritime, and they pressed us to use Le Colombier for holidays. It is best described as five-star camping, for we would have to take our bedding and some other things with us. But there were two habitable buildings, with cooking stoves, proper plumbing and hot water, a shower room, lavatories, all the essential kitchen and china ware, electricity and refrigerators. The whole place was utterly charming, and depended upon our own efforts to add some improvement each year - a chest of drawers, perhaps, or a battle won against encroaching brambles. This was our scene and we loved it.

Against this background, the family were having their ups and downs. Anthony's marriage failed towards the end of 1987. Fifteen months later he married Carole, by which time he had joined the Royal Army Medical Corps (RAMC) and been posted to Celle, north of Hannover. It was a pleasure to go back to RMA Sandhurst again for Anthony's pass-out parade, and to meet his drill sergeants, of whom I had heard plenty of anecdote. They had heard about me, too, and we enjoyed a chat together.

That same summer (1988) Barbara and I went to the States for a long holiday, bouncing off friends on the way. Much of the time was spent in California, but we began near Cape Canaveral. We failed to spot any of the 4,000 alligators allegedly resident in the Kennedy Space Centre, but we did see a space shuttle being transported on its vast tractor vehicle towards its launching pad. It was the first such event following the dreadful accident to Columbia. We were also taken to Orlando to visit the Disney enterprise called EPCOT, which was quite outstanding.

On the way back from California we stayed with friends in Williamsburg. These were the Sunells, who had been seconded to the Fifth Tanks in Fallingbostel many years previously. As might be expected, we were given a blow-by-blow account of the surrender of Cornwallis to Washington after the battle of Yorktown, which is close by. Williamsburg itself is a delightful place and a classic example of the wonderful way in which the USA looks after its heritage. It is a living museum, with shop attendants and others dressed in the appropriate costumes as they go about their business. It can be quite spooky sometimes.

A month or so before Anthony's second marriage in February 1989, James's wife left him, and he has lived with us ever since. I suppose none of us had expected such turmoil, but no family these days seems to escape it. In his own way, Jonathan added to the passage of events by announcing in the summer that he would leave the Army. He plucked up the courage to tell me while we were sipping a beer in the garden one summer day.

This was a bit of a blow but I kept my counsel, except to suggest that the right place to make that decision was at regimental duty and not from the MOD. He was nearing the end of a very successful tour with Operational Requirements, and it happened that the general for whom he worked had been his CO in the First a few years previously. This was Jeremy Blacker, who insisted that Jonathan should indeed return to the regiment in 1990 for at least a year in command of a squadron. At the end of that time, Jonathan had it in writing that, given almost certain promotion, he could expect to get command of the First. It speaks volumes for his resolution that he stuck to his plan and left the Army. That he did so put him ahead of the rush that followed the ending of the Cold War and the beginning of huge redundancies.

Throughout this rather turbulent time I had been involved with Perkins in the planning of a major event. A year or two previously it had been put to me by Perkins that there were some unsettling straws in the wind blowing around the bazaars. There was talk of research into new types of armoured fighting vehicle that seemed to suggest the need for a new design of power pack. Others spoke of the possibility that robot tanks might become viable. The question to be answered was whether Perkins should begin to consider some new ideas of their own as the millennium approached.

My response was to suggest that Perkins should run a full-scale two-day international seminar to help resolve the problem. It would be called PAPUA 21, for Power And Propulsion Under Armour in the 21st century. I had remembered that, during my time in Whitehall, MGO had ordered me to set up a seminar as a means of exchanging information with the captains of industry on the problems of army equipment procurement. It was to be called Exercise Oracle, and it still is, for it has become a major item in the calendar each year. It was a two-day affair based on Shrivenham, involving senior speakers from MOD and industry, and MGO hosted two lunches and a full-scale dinner with all the bells and whistles.

My experience of running Oracle helped me to develop the idea of an international equivalent which Perkins could host, also at Shrivenham. The aim would be to assemble both official and industrial speakers from each of France, Germany, the States and ourselves. I took advice, and put together a list of topics and speakers, being greatly helped by my knowledge of personalities in all four countries. An outline plan evolved and, to Perkins's great credit, they picked up the baton and ran with it. Peter Baker, the director to whom I reported, worked out how to meet the budget, and then chose the date with great care. The Perkins machine went into action, and PAPUA 21 took place in March 1990. It was an outstanding success and earned Perkins much kudos in the international market place. As far as I know, no one else in our defence industry has run such an event, including our big prime contractors.

The bottom line for Perkins was that they felt confident in continuing to pursue the achievement of excellence in the worldwide production and distribution of high-speed diesel engines. The same goes, I think, for their competitors.

My links with other clients continued to wax and wane. I had an interesting two years helping a German tank manufacturer, Krauss Maffei Wehrtechnik of Munich, during their participation in the international competition for the replacement of the Chieftain tank. I was not so much a lobbyist as an adviser and interpreter of our procurement system. The Leopard 2 tank was, in my opinion, the most favoured alternative to our own Challenger 2, which ultimately won the competition and is now beginning to enter service.

Meanwhile, Jonathan had emerged into the wild and woolly world, and was trying to convince the Banque National de Paris (BNP) that, while he knew nothing about banking and very little French, they needed him. The response was a series of Gallic shrugs and, losing patience, he responded to one of the companies in GEC-Marconi who were after him. He joined them in the spring of 1991, and almost immediately found himself briefing his erstwhile CO and Whitehall employer, General Jeremy Blacker, on the efficacies of a Marconi product. A couple of months later, BNP suddenly decided they needed Jonathan after all. He was much perturbed at having to leave Marconi after so short a time, but they were very kind to him. As he left their Leicester offices, he said, 'You could do worse than employ my father' - and they did.

Settling down in a village takes time. For several years we felt that our centre of gravity had scarcely moved from the Old Vicarage, just ten miles away as the crow flies. Continuity came from our involvement with horsey events and with the shoot at Shrivenham. It took five years for the local branch of the Royal British Legion to brace themselves sufficiently to cope with a general. When they discovered that I was a fairly normal human being, they decided to make me chairman, and we began to enjoy the feeling of having some sort of involvement in the village. For some time I was president as well, until at last we found an excellent chairman to take over from me. I have the honour still to remain their president.

On a different level came my involvement with an amenity society concerned with the Cotswold Water Park. This is a stretch of wetland amounting to more than a hundred lakes, the aftermath of many years of gravel extraction along the border between Gloucestershire and Wiltshire. There had been a proposal to site a huge holiday village on a most inappropriate site, and the Villages Society had emerged as a focus for objection. This has been my only involvement with local politics, apart from an interest in the work of CPRE, and now I know why it is not my scene. The Public Inquiry went in favour of the holiday village, and it is a strange irony that it was never built. It seems that we were right after all, but it took six years for the planning world to recognize formally the demise of a wholly misguided project, at great expense to the ratepayer.

Much more civilized has been my involvement as a trustee of the Malmesbury Community Trust, my appointment having come about as a resident of one of the outlying villages in the so-called 'area of benefit'. I render service as a de facto chairman on behalf of the mayor.

A new dimension entered our lives in February 1991 when our first granddaughter was born, and continued delightfully through to May 1994, when a fourth granddaughter appeared on the scene. Quite clearly Nature has been concerned to restore the balance against our own three sons. Alexandra, Daisy, Georgia and Sophie took a long time coming, it seemed to us, but at last we have come to experience the joy of being grandparents.

Our horsey involvements fill the calendar. It is an arcane process that gets one established on a list of fence judges. It is always a different list for each event, and seems to be a matter of 'dead men's shoes'. We are on the list for Dauntsey and Gatcombe, and have just begun at Savernake. We are also on the list for pony club events in both the VWH and the Beaufort.

Timekeeping is the other thing, emerging largely out of my activities with tetrathlon. Barbara and I, with our son James and other friends, make up an experienced team of timekeepers. Favourite events are the VWH Team Chase, and the inter-hunt Silver Fox Challenge which complements the recently established Marlborough Cup - a three-mile race over solid timber near Barbury Castle.

Each year we visit the Badminton Horse Trials, less than twenty miles away, and almost invariably take a late summer break to the Burghley Horse Trials near Stamford - perhaps our favourite. As my consultancy business draws finally to a close, these horsey things constitute happy milestones in our lives. More than this, we even got into horse ownership for a while. Barbara's hunting days had come to an end, and we bought a six-month-old, part-bred Cleveland Bay. Barbara's first impression was of a little ragamuffin and we called him The Muffin Man. Barbara wanted the interest of bringing him on, and he surprised us all by growing into a wonderful 17-hand animal with great presence and a most engaging disposition. He would often make us laugh and everyone who saw him fell in love with him. We were delighted when he won the national working hunter championship at the Cleveland Bay Show, bringing us some silver plate to hang on the bannisters.

We committed him to the eventing world in the hands of an excellent young jockey called Jonty Evans, who had trained with Andrew Nicholson. He was doing brilliantly until he had a bad accident at a novice event. Muffin came out unscathed but Jonty was badly hurt. The outcome was that we sold Muffin to a happy home, being unable to afford him any more. But he had given us much joy.

Then the arrival of grandchildren gave us the urge to buy a mischievous Welsh pony of diminutive size and considerable character. His chief claim to fame was the ability to get himself outside any fence that was meant to contain him. He was called Charlie Gee, and now lives in the Peak District which probably suits him better.

Our field and paddock are now graced by a neighbour's cows, and our stable block is out of commission. Old Megan, my spaniel, is kept very fit by Barbara's one-year-old springer called Chime - a little dog of immense character and energy. We shall have to introduce her to the shoot before long where, after twenty-five years or so, I have finally become one of the syndicate leaders.

Jonathan has long since left BNP, and works for a small merchant bank that operates in the world of mines and quarries. He travels everywhere from Australia to Arizona at a moment's notice, and works very hard. Anthony, also, has long since left the RAMC, and has mastered the exams that made him a Member of the Royal College of Obstetricians and Gynaecologists, and is now engaged in research. Both he and Carole work very hard too. James is working on a business plan to start up a small business of his own, and we wish him well.

We have discovered how fortunate we are to live on the fringe of this village, which is very much a going concern. There is an excellent primary school, a garage that sells things, and a village shop that truly does have one of everything. Because the village exists in two distinct communities, one surrounding the church and the other around the old station, there are two post offices. One of these is the second village shop, and the other post office has things to sell too. There are three pubs of very different character, and many businesses. These include a thriving printer, a hairdresser, a domestic heating oil distributor, a supplier of conservatories, and several building enterprises. There are some fine playing fields, and the sports association enjoy their own pavilion. There is even a squash court. We are about 1,500 souls, making a relatively large community, and we live right out in the boondocks.

The time of the VE Day celebrations in May 1995 was a revelation. About nine weeks beforehand, I was rung up by our Legion Standard Bearer. He told me that people in the village were getting together about VE Day, and they had all thought it right that the Royal British Legion should take the lead. I agreed wholeheartedly.

'Right,' I was told. 'You're chairing a meeting in the Sports Pavilion in three nights' time.'

They were all there, from the Mother's and Toddler's Group to the Twinning Association, from the Pétanque Club to the Rugby Club, from the Primary School to the Mothers' Union, and so on. They explained what they wanted to have happen on VE Day, and we (the Legion, that is) told them it would probably cost about £2,000. The Parish Council immediately donated £750, and we took it from there. I suggested that we did not intend to make a profit, but that if there were funds left over, could these go towards that year's Poppy Appeal? Of course.

What actually happened on VE Day was as follows. The bar opened at 4 p.m. in a large striped marquee. At 4.30 a Hercules from RAF Lyneham provided a flypast for the benefit of the small children, who were formed into a human VE and waved their flags. The children spent the next hour having a Teddy Bear's Picnic with an entertainer, and then at 5.30 released a cloud of balloons for a balloon race.

Apart from the bar, there was something of a pause while folk took the opportunity to get a bite at home and put babies to bed. By 7 p.m. the sports field was filling up again, and the mother of all barbecues was swinging into action. At £1 a head and 50p for children it offered superb value. At 7.30 there was an aerobatic display by a local pilot. By this time some 700 people must have gathered, and it was the Legion's turn to perform: I took station beneath the flagpole and introduced a fifteen-minute CD which a neighbour of mine, Peter Hornby, had produced. We had the right snatches of music like Elgar's 'Nimrod', stuff from the last night of the Proms and so on. We had Alvar Liddell saying, 'We interrupt the Home Service to announce that the Prime Minister will address the nation . . .' and the voice of Churchill giving his 'finest hour' speech; Churchill again, speaking to the crowds in Whitehall fifty years before. Then came the Evening Hymn, which includes the Last Post, and our D-Day veteran lowered the flag. Finally the national anthem, and a few wet cheeks.

As a complete contrast we were then swept into action by a combination of the church choir and the local glee group, and song sheets were quickly distributed. We did it all, from Chattanooga Choo Choo to Run Rabbit Run, 700 full-throated voices giving their best. This lasted twenty-five minutes, until I was able to announce that the Queen was about to lead the nation from Hyde Park in two minutes' silence. You could have heard a pin drop. Then we lit a huge beacon, built for the price of a bottle of whisky, there was a big raffle, and then a quite magnificent firework display.

The village was proud of itself, and rightly so. They gave us nearly £1,300 pounds for the Poppy Appeal.

There is so much to look forward to yet. We have joined a syndicate owning another splendid young event horse, and Jonty Evans is our jockey again. The horse celebrated the new venture by winning his novice section at his first ever two-day event. Not bad, even if we do own only a fetlock.